The (Not Too Serious) Grammar, Punctuation, and Style Guide to Legal Writing

The (Not Too Serious) Grammar, Punctuation, and Style Guide to Legal Writing

Diana J. Simon

Associate Clinical Professor of Law
University of Arizona
James E. Rogers College of Law

CAROLINA ACADEMIC PRESS

Durham, North Carolina

ISBN   978-1-5310-2477-2
e-ISBN   978-1-5310-2478-9
LCCN   2022029409

See catalog.loc.gov for complete
Library of Congress Cataloging-in-Publication Data

Carolina Academic Press
700 Kent Street
Durham, North Carolina 27701
(919) 489-7486
www.cap-press.com

Printed in the United States of America
2023 Printing

Contents

....

Preface

....

When the publisher asked me the impetus for writing this book, I realized there were three. And even if there were more than three, because of the magic associated with the number three (see Chapter 12 on transitions and the magic of three), I would not include them.

First, because all writing is autobiographical, this book is my life story. You might wonder how rules about grammar, punctuation, and writing style can be autobiographical. I will tell you. My mother taught English and journalism, and she believed she was put on this planet to correct my grammatical and punctuation errors. From an early age, she would ask me something like, "You call this a sentence?" I think I was five, and I did not even know what a sentence was, so my response was something like this: "I don't know." The point is that at an early age I turned my back on grammar and punctuation. I simply did not see the point especially because, by the time I was in elementary school, I was too busy being a secret agent. Grammar and punctuation were not going to help me uncover some international plot to overthrow the government.[1]

Second, I have come to realize that good legal writing is not divorced from good grammar, punctuation, and writing style. They go hand in hand. Indeed, as soon as I started teaching legal writing, some 12 years ago, it became clear to me that, as much as I wanted to, I could no longer be indifferent to these topics. As I reviewed countless memos and briefs my students wrote, there it was, like a bright, flashing neon sign—"you call this a sentence?" But I also noticed that, like my five-year-old self

---

1. In law school, I thought I wanted to join the FBI until I went to the first informational meeting and found out I had to do approximately 14 pushups in a minute. After that, I had to pursue other career alternatives.

(and well beyond), my students did not see the point of mastering proper grammar and punctuation; their minds were on finishing law school and then creating a more just world (and maybe a few were intent on becoming secret agents). That got me thinking—there must be a better way to learn this information.

Third, the telling of stories is the best way to convey information. Cognitive scientists and legal writing professors agree: storytelling engages readers and makes information more memorable.[2] This is even true with abstract legal rules. You can create rule stories, and "telling the rule's life story can be the most memorable, engaging, and persuasive tool in your belt. Rule stories just beg to be read."[3]

And believe it or not, there are stories to be told about grammar and punctuation. As (I hope) you will agree after reading this book, by telling a story about the serial comma, for example, it becomes more memorable. While some researchers disagree that rules about grammar or punctuation can be learned with stories,[4] these researchers, who are not lawyers, may not realize that lawyers and law students learn about a lot of dry topics with the help of stories (Let's face it—topics like contract damages or a statute of limitations has never been a real conversation starter.) I am one of those people that respectfully disagrees with the impossibility of story in grammar and style.

This textbook is my attempt to tell some of those stories that I had wished my mother had told me—to use imagination, creativity, and at times humor[5] to tell stories about abstract rules of punctuation, grammar, and writing style. The point is to have a little fun or there is no point.

---

2. *See, e.g.*, Ruth Anne Robbins, *Create a Portal for Story Immersion*, 18 Legal Comm. & Rhetoric: JALWD 27 (2021).

3. Joseph Regalia, *A Plaintiff and a Defendant Walk into a Bar: Simple Tools for Telling Stories in Your Legal Writing*, L. Professor Blogs Network: App. Advoc. Blog (Apr. 13, 2019), https://lawprofessors.typepad.com/appellate_advocacy/2019/04/storytelling-short-and-dirty.html.

4. Roger C. Schank & Robert P. Adelson, *Knowledge and Memory: The Real Story*, *in* Knowledge and Memory: The Real Story 1, 16 (Robert S. Wyer, Jr., ed., 1995).

5. I also wanted to be a standup comic until I realized that that would mean I would have to starve for many years and maybe forever.

Now that you know the why, you need to know the who—the people who helped me with this book. I want to thank my husband, Don Tringali, who is my biggest fan (and critic) because he reviewed every word of this book and encouraged me every step of the way. I want to thank my student, Liam Martin, who also reviewed every word of this book, made sure the citations were correct, and gave me valuable feedback as a member of the audience for which I am writing. Moreover, thanks goes to Tim Eigo, the editor of the *Arizona Attorney*, for being the first person to read and publish my first article on a punctuation issue—the semicolon—and praise my voice and creativity. Further, I want to give credit to my colleagues—Sylvia Lett, Susie Salmon, and Tessa Dysart—for not only their encouragement but acting as a sounding board for me throughout the writing process. Additionally, I want to thank my brother, Scott Simon, for reading my article and suggesting I author a book full of related articles, and John Konrad, who created all of the cartoons for the book, providing much-needed laughter throughout the process. Last, but certainly not least, I want to thank my editors at Carolina Academic Press, David Herzig and Ryland Bowman, for saying yes to publishing the book and for their support and encouragement along the way.

The (Not Too Serious) Grammar, Punctuation, and Style Guide to Legal Writing

1

Why This Matters

L ike you, I did not go to law school to learn grammar and punctuation. That was beneath me, as I was sure I had already learned all the grammar and punctuation I needed to know. I went to law school to save the world; other than that, my plans were up in the air. And I certainly could not see a relationship between saving the world and proper placement of a comma.

I also did not realize when I entered law school that being a lawyer means you will (no ifs, ands, or buts) be required to write. In fact, in a study done by the National Conference of Bar Examiners, newly licensed attorneys from across the country were surveyed and asked how significant written communication was to their performance.[1] A score of 4, the highest score, meant "extremely" important, and *100%* of the attorneys surveyed reported that they engaged in written communication. Written communication received an overall score of 3.77, higher than *any* other activity. The second highest score, 3.67, was for "paying attention to the details."[2] Therefore, rest assured that you will be called upon to write as a lawyer, and the details matter.

Based upon my experience both practicing and teaching legal skills, there is one thing I can say with certainty—learning grammar, punctuation, and other style issues is essential to good legal writing and therefore to being a good lawyer. These are not just silly rules that no one really cares about: I can assure you people *do* care—*a lot*. As you will

---

1. Susan M. Case, *The Testing Column: The NCBE Job Analysis: A Study of the Newly Licensed Lawyer*, THE BAR EXAMINER, 52-56 (March 2013), https://www.ncbex.org/assets/media_files/Bar-Examiner/articles/2013/820113testingcolumn.pdf.

2. *Id.* at 55.

learn from this book, there are many reasons people care about your grammar and punctuation and many reasons you should care.

First, in case you are thinking, I got this, think again. In my experience, most students come to law school thinking they will be effective legal writers right off the bat because they got As on all their papers in college, especially those who were English or history majors (or a similar major requiring students to write lots of papers). Then, they get their first piece of legal writing back from their legal writing professor with substantial comments. Where once they were praised, these students are now condemned.[3] And they think, something must be wrong with that writing professor.

The problem is that legal writing, while like other kinds of writing in some ways, is unlike other writing in many other ways. Whereas professors in college may have rewarded you for expressiveness when writing about your experiences, your originality, or for conveying your feelings, legal writing professors will reward you instead for your accuracy, brevity, and clarity. Each word matters, and attention to detail is critical.

Legal writing professors care a lot about grammar, punctuation, and other writing rules because these are some key ingredients of effective legal writing. Perhaps surprisingly (or perhaps not), law professors generally complain that their students cannot write—and do not understand basic grammar, punctuation, and capitalization.[4] Therefore, if you can master these basic skills, then not only will you improve your writing, but your legal writing professor will be pleased. And one of your goals in life should be to please your legal writing professor. You heard it here first.

Aside from your legal writing professor, two other categories of people who will care deeply about your writing are lawyers (including your supervisors) and judges. In a survey of practitioners and judges (as well as legal writing professors), all agreed that after compliance with the court rules, including word limits, what mattered most in legal writing

---

3. Bryan Garner, *Do Law Students Become Worse Writers?*, ABA for Law Students: Student Lawyer (May 1, 2013), https://abaforlawstudents.com/2013/05/01/law-students-become-worse-writers/.

4. Ann L. Nowak, *Tough Love: The Law School that Required Its Students to Learn Good Grammar*, 28 Touro L. Rev. 1369, 1369 (2012).

was that there be no grammar mistakes.[5] Further, a recent survey of more than a thousand state and federal judges revealed that they have very strong views not only on substantive issues but on style and punctuation matters, including issues like the use of quotations (Chapter 9) and the use of the serial comma (Chapter 4).[6]

Of course, it is not just about what the surveys show: real cases have been won or lost because of punctuation or grammar. Big money has changed hands because of the placement of a comma. You will learn about these cases in different chapters of this book.

And if you are thinking, well, I am never going to court, you should know that it is not just lawyers who go to court (litigators) who are impacted. Lawyers who negotiate and draft contracts (transactional attorneys), or who draft legislation, must also have command of grammar and punctuation rules.

Most legal writing "is a species of persuasive writing,"[7] and using proper grammar and punctuation is essential to persuading your reader.[8] Some of you may have learned about Aristotle's modes of persuasion: ethos, pathos, and logos. If you have not, that's fine, as most legal writing professors will cover this with you when you learn about persuasive writing. Ethos refers to persuading your reader through the credibility and character of your reader. Pathos refers to an appeal made to an audience's emotions to evoke feeling. Logos means persuading the reader by making a logical argument.

When you introduce yourself to an audience through your writing (whether to a lawyer, a client, or a judge), your audience will judge your believability and even your trustworthiness—in other words, your ethos—through your "command of the rules of grammar, usage, and

---

5. Susan Hanley Kosse & David T. ButleRitchie, *How Judges, Practitioners, and Legal Writing Teachers Assess the Writing Skills of New Law Graduates: A Comparative Study*, 53 J. Legal Educ. 80, 90 (2003).

6. Ross Guberman, *Judges Speaking Softly: What They Long for When They Read*, Litigation, Summer 2018, at 48, 48, 51–52.

7. Garner, *supra* note 3.

8. Lillian B. Hardwick, *Classical Persuasion through Grammar and Punctuation*, 3 J. Ass'n Legal Writing Dirs. 75, 75 (2006).

punctuation."[9] Therefore, if your command of these items is poor, your reader will be left with a bad first impression, and, as we all know, bad first impressions are difficult to correct.[10]

Improper grammar and punctuation can also produce a negative emotional response in your audience.[11] When a lawyer writes, it is not like writing to a friend; your audience is hostile and skeptical. Therefore, if your writing detracts from the clarity of your message, your audience will be alienated.[12] In fact, although it may seem unfair, if punctuation or grammatical mistakes are made, the reader will think either consciously or unconsciously that this inattention to detail is like a contagious disease that extends to other substantive aspects of your writing, such as your analysis.

These errors can also impact your ability to construct a cogent and persuasive argument—its logos—because your reader might be confused or, even worse, misled. For example, in a case arising in North Dakota, the defendant argued that a sworn statement attempting to prove the credibility of an informant had been misleading.[13] The problem was that the statement contained various typos resulting in an inaccurate description of the informant's background. The problematic portion of the statement stated that the informant "has answered questions truthfully on incident's [sic] that have happened almost a year ago" and "has testified under oath in a [sic] jury trials on the cases involving several narcotics users."[14] The problem was the statement, with its typos, indicated that the witness had helped on more than one occasion, when the truth was, she had testified at only one trial previously. The court held that the statement, because of its bad grammar and typos, had "misled the magistrate" who signed the search warrant. Thus, the sworn statement did not achieve its purpose; it did not establish the credibility of the informant, and the court suppressed the evidence obtained from the

---

9. *See id.* at 77 (citing Michael R. Smith, Advanced Legal Writing: Theories & Strategies in Persuasive Writing 164 (2002)).

10. *See id.* at 77–78.

11. *Id.* at 99.

12. *Id.* at 98.

13. *Id.* at 86 (discussing State v. Donovan, 688 N.W.2d 646 (N.D. 2004)); *Donovan,* 688 N.W.2d at 649.

14. *Id.* at 86–87.

search.[15] This was not just a court's emotional reaction; it significantly impacted the prosecutor's case.

There will be many other examples in this book illustrating negative consequences resulting from a lawyer making grammar or punctuation mistakes in a piece of legal writing. As you dive into the chapters that follow—and find yourself, at times, tempted to scream who cares?—just keep reminding yourself that *you* should: because this stuff matters.

---

15. *Donovan,* 688 N.W.2d at 652.

2

Harry Potter and
the Sinful Comma Splice

U pon reading that title, you might be wondering if there was a Harry Potter book you missed. No, there wasn't. But I blame Harry Potter (not him individually, of course, but the series) for an issue I often see in students' writing: the dreaded comma splice. When my first-year students are feeling overwhelmed by the sheer number of new rules and issues they must learn, they will ask, "What if we can remember only one rule involving punctuation or grammar? What would that be?" My standard answer is, "You have to pay attention to all of these things, but if you can only remember a single rule, avoid comma splices." That is when they look at me and wonder if I just landed from some other planet.

But truth be told, I never even heard of the term "comma splice" until I started teaching legal writing. In my sheltered world before teaching, as a hard-nosed litigator in an entertainment firm in Los Angeles, a sentence that had a comma splice was a "run-on sentence."[1] For students and other readers who are still leading sheltered lives, this phenomenon is called a comma splice because a comma is used to "splice together two

---

1. The conclusion that a sentence containing an improper comma splice is a form of a run-on sentence is apparently controversial. Bryan Garner would agree that grammarians consider a sentence containing a comma splice "a form of run-on sentence." BRYAN A. GARNER, THE REDBOOK: A MANUAL ON LEGAL STYLE, 5 (4th ed. 2018) [hereinafter REDBOOK]. But Mignon Fogarty, the *New York Times*-bestselling author of *Grammar Girl's Quick and Dirty Tips for Better Writing*, disagrees and says that "[r]un-on sentences are, in some ways, the opposite of comma splices; instead of using the wrong punctuation, they occur when you don't use any punctuation between two sentences." MIGNON FOGARTY, GRAMMAR GIRL'S QUICK AND DIRTY TIPS FOR BETTER WRITING 106 (2008). We will leave for another day the answer to this pivotal question.

complete sentences when that isn't the function of a comma."[2] (At some point, I would like to meet the person who coined the term "comma splice" because it nails the problem perfectly.)

Wide use of comma splices is a relatively recent phenomenon. While it is difficult to find statistics tracking the usage of comma splices over time, I can assure you that over my years of teaching (and not just legal writing but other classes as well), there has been a dramatic increase.

And in case you doubt my observations, then perhaps you will believe Bryan Garner, one of the leading authorities on the English language in legal writing circles. In an interview with him about actual data on the use of English language and language changes over time, he had this to say about comma splices: "[m]ore and more people are communicating with comma splices—perhaps in text messages and in email messages—and it could be that comma splices will soon be somehow considered standard. I don't think so—I would say over my dead body."[3]

The next natural question of course is "why?" Many theories abound, but I find support for one theory in the graph I have created on the following page.

While this graph might not be based entirely (or at all) on empirical evidence, you catch my drift. Comma splice usage has increased a lot.[4]

As stated above, my working theory, as depicted on the graph below (and utterly lacking in actual proof) is that the culprit is Harry Potter. Now, before you complain to my publisher because you think I am attacking your favorite book series, let me be clear: I loved the Harry Potter books. I read every one of them, and I have seen every movie based on the books. But one must follow "the facts."

---

2. FOGARTY, *supra* note 1, at 104.

3. Daniel McMahon, *A Conversation with the World's Leading Authority on the English Language About Big Data, Google Ngrams, and Language Change*, BUS. INSIDER, (Apr. 30, 2016, 9:03 AM), https://www.businessinsider.com/bryan-garner-interview-english-usage-google-ngrams-big-data-2016-4 ; *see also* Ben Yagoda, *The Most Comma Mistakes*, N.Y. TIMES (May 21, 2012, 9:17 PM), https://opinionator.blogs.nytimes.com/2012/05/21/the-most-comma-mistakes/ ("When I started teaching at the University of Delaware some years ago, I was positively gobsmacked by the multitude of comma splices that confronted me. They have not abated.").

4. To be precise, by "a lot," I mean a "whole lot."

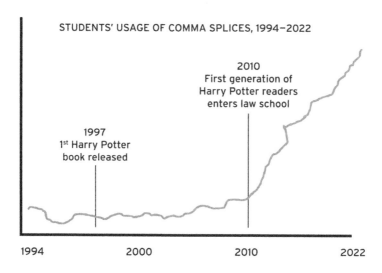

STUDENTS' USAGE OF COMMA SPLICES, 1994–2022

2010
First generation of
Harry Potter readers
enters law school

1997
1st Harry Potter
book released

1994   2000   2010   2022

The first Harry Potter book, *Harry Potter and the Philosopher's Stone*, was published in 1997,[5] and the last one, *Harry Potter and the Deathly Hallows*, was published in 2007.[6] Having sold 500 million copies worldwide, it is the best-selling book series in history.[7] While Harry Potter is for all audiences, from a technical perspective, the series is categorized as a middle-grade read, which typically encompasses 9-to-12-year-olds.[8] That means that, on average, the first Harry Potter readers entered law school about 2010, and my very unscientific study suggests that 2010 corresponds to the time when comma splices started their reign of terror.

5. J.K. ROWLING, HARRY POTTER AND THE PHILOSOPHER'S STONE (1997). It was not published in the United States until 1998, and thus, the chart above might be off by a year but is otherwise perfectly accurate.

6. J.K. ROWLING, HARRY POTTER AND THE DEATHLY HALLOWS (2007).

7. *List of Best-selling Books*, WIKIPEDIA, https://en.wikipedia.org/wiki/List_of_best-selling_books (last visited Mar. 24, 2022).

8. Jen Harper, *When Is Your Kid Ready for Harry Potter? A Guide for Getting Started*, BARNES & NOBLE: B&N READS (Jan. 21, 2016, 11:00 AM), https://www.barnesandnoble.com/blog/kids/is-your-kid-old-enough-for-harry-potter-a-guide-for-getting-started/. For more in-depth statistics on the target audience for the book series, *see* Kate Palmer, *Potter Fans More Likely to Read Rowling's Latest Release*, YOUGOVAMERICA (Aug. 2, 2013, 7:55 AM), https://today.yougov.com/topics/lifestyle/articles-reports/2013/08/02/20130731-potter. This article says that while millennial men are the most likely to have picked up a Potter book at one point, they are the least likely to have finished the entire series; in contrast, women in the 18–34 category were more likely to have finished the entire series. *Id.*

If you are scratching your head at this point trying to figure out what Harry Potter has to do with comma splices, you apparently have not heard that the author, J.K. Rowling, has been called "Queen of the Comma Splice."[9] In fact, many English teachers have taken issue with Rowling's improper grammar generally and use of comma splices specifically.[10] Some have gone so far as to count the number of comma splices in her books (I know you are curious, so I will tell you: 474 run-on sentences in *Harry Potter and the Deathly Hallows*).[11] For example, Hermione, the last person you would expect to use comma splices, says this in *Harry Potter and the Deathly Hallows*: "It's just a morality tale, it's obvious which gift is best, which one you'd choose—."[12] Another author points to *Harry Potter and the Order of the Phoenix* as further proof of Rowling's comma splice issues and notes that over the course of 870 pages, she uses comma splices frequently, even though "thousands of young, impressionable readers take this in [and then go to law school and use them there] as they valiantly succeed in reading that book from cover to cover."[13] Thus, based on the evidence, the root of the comma splice explosion stems from the Harry Potter books.

A. Short History and Explanation of the Comma Splice

Now that we have identified the root cause of the dramatic uptick in comma splice usage, it is time to go back and understand what a comma splice is. A comma splice is defined as "the use of a comma between coordinate main clauses not connected by a conjunction (as in 'nobody

---

9. Ryan-Tyler N. Mason, *King of the Comma Splice*, Random Thoughts from a Nonlinear Mind (Jan. 22, 2021), https://rtnmblog.com/king-of-the-comma-splice/.

10. *E.g.,id.*; Alan Warhaftig, *No Wizat Grammar*, Educ. Wk. (Sept. 24, 2007), https://www.edweek.org/teaching-learning/opinion-no-wiz-at-grammar/2007/09; Walter H. Johnson, *The Sentence-Structure Dilemma*, Eng. J., Jan. 2006, at 14, 14–15; Paul Livesey, *Harry Potter and the Pedants*, Tes (Jul. 25, 2003, 1:00 AM), https://www.tes.com/magazine/archive/harry-potter-and-the-pedants-0; Katie May, *Harry Potter and the Comma Splice*, Nitpicker's Nook (Dec. 5, 2010), https://nitpickersnook.wordpress.com/2010/12/05/harry-potter-and-the-comma-splice/.

11. Warhaftig, *supra* note 10.

12. *Id.* (citing Harry Potter and the Deathly Hallows, *supra* note 6, at 414).

13. Johnson, *supra* note 10, at 14.

goes there anymore, it's boring')."[14] The first known use of the term was in 1924.[15] They have been called many other names but most of them are pejorative: comma fault, a horror, a nightmare, insidious germs, comma error, or comma blunder.[16]

While today's grammarians eschew comma splices, this was not always the case. In the eighteenth century, when the average life expectancy was 25–40 years,[17] punctuation was less important, probably because people had more important things to worry about—like surviving. Well-known authors from that time used comma splices frequently, including Benjamin Franklin and Jonathan Swift.[18]

And ironically, even in the twentieth century, although *Strunk & White* says not to join independent clauses with a comma,[19] E.B. White himself (the "White" in *Strunk & White*), in a letter written in 1963, wrote, "Tell Johnny to read Santayana for a little while, it will improve his sentence structure."[20]

Even today, many writers think this focus on comma splices is absurd. They see this attack on comma splices as a form of elitism, arguing there is nothing inherently wrong or abhorrent about using them.[21] As one English professor opined regarding the attack on comma splices, "it's just

---

14. *Comma splice*, MERRIAM-WEBSTER, https://www.merriam-webster.com/dictionary/comma%20splice (last visited Mar. 24, 2022).

15. *Id.*

16. Irene Teoh Brosnahan, *A Few Good Words for the Comma Splice*, COLL. ENG., Oct. 1976, at 184, 184–88, https://www.jstor.org/stable/376343; Gabe Doyle, *Comma Splices: Historical and Informal, Not Wrong*, MOTIVATED GRAMMAR (July 23, 2012), https://motivatedgrammar.wordpress.com/2012/07/23/comma-splices-historical-and-informal-not-wrong/.

17. *Life Expectancy*, WIKIPEDIA, https://en.wikipedia.org/wiki/Life_expectancy (last visited Mar. 24, 2022).

18. *Comma Splices: What They Are and How to Correct Them (or Not)*, MERRIAM-WEBSTER: WORDS AT PLAY, https://www.merriam-webster.com/words-at-play/maybe-you-like-comma-splices-maybe-you-dont (last visited Mar. 24, 2022). For example, Jonathan Swift wrote in *Polite Conversation*, "Why, sure Betty, thou art bewitcht, this Cream is burnt too." And Benjamin Franklin wrote in *Autobiography*, "The New Jersey job was obtained, I contrived a copperplate press for it."

19. WILLIAM STRUNK, JR. & E. B. WHITE, THE ELEMENTS OF STYLE 5–7 (4th ed., Longman 1999).

20. Doyle, *supra* note 16.

21. *Id.*; *see* Brosnahan, *supra* note 16, at 184, 188.

a useful tool for the implementation of power, a way that English instructors have found of establishing and protecting their own prestige."[22]

But maybe because I teach formal legal writing and fall into the camp that believes comma splices are bad, I remain dedicated to eradicating their use. Accordingly, below we will learn how to recognize a comma splice and how to reconstruct the sentence, a lesson apparently not learned at Hogwarts.

B. Courts Care About Them

But before doing that, I think you need to be persuaded that courts care about comma splices. And, of course, they do, or I would not have mentioned it. In *Anderson v. Western National Mutual Insurance Company*,[23] a federal district court in South Dakota addressed the standard for a bad faith claim against an insurance company.[24] In doing so, it turned to a decision of the South Dakota Supreme Court but had this to say about that court's use of a comma splice when articulating the standard, rendering the standard unclear and confusing: "The published version of the *Champion* case unfortunately... employed a comma splice in a key passage creating a confusing standard."[25] Here is how the South Dakota Supreme Court stated the standard using a comma splice:

> [F]or proof of bad faith, there must be an absence of a reasonable basis for denial of policy benefits *and* the knowledge or reckless disregard of a reasonable basis for denial, implicit in that test is our conclusion that the knowledge of the lack of a reasonable basis may be inferred... where there is a reckless disregard of a lack of a reasonable basis for denial....[26]

Did you spot the improper comma splice? Anyone? It appears right before the word *implicit*. But do not worry. In a later case, the Supreme

---

22. Anne L. Klinck, *Unravelling the Comma Splice*, ENG. J., Mar. 1998, at 96, 96–98 (internal quotation marks and citation omitted).

23. 857 F. Supp. 2d 896 (D.S.D. 2012).

24. *Id.* at 903.

25. *Id.*

26. *Id.* at 903 n.9 (quoting Champion v. U.S. Fid. & Guar. Co., 399 N.W.2d 320, 324 (S.D. 1987)).

Court of South Dakota restated the standard and inserted a period after denial and then capitalized the "I" in *implicit*.[27] It's not just lawyers and law students who make mistakes—and learn from them.

C. Examples of Comma Splices and How to Fix Them

Now that we know why comma splices are on the rise and that legal writing experts and the courts care about that, let's turn to more examples of comma splices and advice on avoiding them.

An improper comma splice is used to join two independent clauses with a comma alone.[28] An "independent clause" is a subject-verb construction that could stand alone as a complete sentence.[29]

Here are some examples:

1. A monsoon has hit Arizona, my house is leaking.
2. It is so wet and rainy, the mosquitoes are out in record numbers.
3. It's the way I am wired, I'm not going to change now.
4. The weather is great today, however, it is going to rain tomorrow.
5. Fall is coming soon, the leaves are already turning yellow and orange.

There are several easy fixes for an improper comma splice. You can: (1) replace the comma with a semicolon; (2) use a coordinating conjunction after the comma; (3) break the clauses into separate sentences; (4) make one of the clauses dependent by introducing it with a subordinate conjunction; or (5) use an em dash.[30]

Let's take each one of these solutions in turn:

---

27. *Id.* at 904 (quoting Dakota, Minn. & E. R.R. v. Acuity, 771 N.W.2d 623, 629 (S.D. 2009)).

28. REDBOOK, *supra* note 1, at 5.

29. *Id.* Daniel McMahon, *The World's Top Grammarian Fears that This Punctuation Error Is Becoming Standard English*, BUS. INSIDER (May 2, 2016, 9:21 AM), https://www. businessinsider.com/comma-splice-2016-4.

30. *Id.*

- *Replace the comma with a semicolon.* For semicolon worshippers, this is one fix. While a comma will not work to join two independent clauses without a conjunction, a semicolon will. It works especially well if you want a strong break in the sentence.[31]

Example with Improper Comma Splice: The Fourteenth Amendment prohibits states from depriving persons of their property without due process of law, it does not define those property interests.

Example with semicolon: The Fourteenth Amendment prohibits states from depriving persons of their property without due process of law; it does not define those property interests.

- *Use a coordinating conjunction after the comma.* The main coordinating conjunctions are "and," "but," "for," "or," "nor," "yet," and "so."[32] They join words or phrases of equal importance.[33]

Example with Improper Comma Splice: The Fourteenth Amendment prohibits states from depriving persons of their property without due process of law, it does not define those property interests.

Example with Coordinating Conjunction: The Fourteenth Amendment prohibits states from depriving persons of their property without due process of law, but it does not define those property interests.

- *Break the clauses into two and create two different sentences.*

Example: The Fourteenth Amendment prohibits states from depriving persons of their property without due process of law. It does not define those property interests.

---

31. REDBOOK, *supra* note 1, at 15.
32. *Id.* at 235.
33. *Id.*

- *Add a subordinate conjunction.* The main subordinate conjunctions are "although," "as," "because," "if," "so,"[34] "since," "that," "unless," and "while."[35] They typically join dependent clauses to independent clauses.[36]

  Example: The Fourteenth Amendment prohibits states from depriving persons of their property without due process of law, although it does not define those property interests.

- *Use an em dash instead of the comma.*[37]

  Example: The Fourteenth Amendment prohibits states from depriving persons of their property without due process of law—it does not define those property interests.

Therefore, there are many ways to fix a sentence containing a comma splice.

D. Exceptions to the No Comma Splice Rule

But there is a twist. There are exceptions to the "comma splices are always bad" rule. Garner provides that in "informal writing, a comma alone may join two short and closely related independent clauses despite the general grammatical disfavor toward the comma splice."[38] He gives this example: "Try it, you'll like it."[39] Similarly, *Strunk & White* allows the use of a comma to separate two independent clauses "when the clauses are very short and alike in form, or when the tone of the sentence

---

34. Careful readers will notice that "so" is listed as both a coordinating and a subordinating conjunction. For an excellent discussion of when so is being used as a coordinating conjunction or a subordinating conjunction, *see* Neal Whitman, *'So' and 'so that': Coordinating or Subordinating Conjunctions?* Quick & Dirty Tips (April 29, 2019), https://www.quickanddirtytips.com/education/grammar/so-and-so-that-coordinating-or-subordinating-conjunctions.

35. Redbook, *supra* note 1, at 236–37.

36. *Id.*

37. *Id.* at 42–43.

38. *Id.* at 16.

39. *Id.*

is easy and conversational."[40] The example provided is "Man proposes, God disposes."[41]

Not only are there exceptions, but the comma splice can be an effective rhetorical device, and some non-legal writing experts have gone so far as to suggest that use of comma splices should not be relegated to some exception to the rule but instead have fashioned an independent rule governing proper usage.[42] One English professor went so far as to formulate an actual test for when a comma splice is acceptable.

Here it is:

> RULE: The comma alone is used to separate independent clauses, without any accompanying conjunction, under the following conditions:
>
> 1. Syntax—the clauses are short and usually parallel in structure though they can be in any combination of affirmative and negative clauses.
> 2. Semantics—the sentence cannot be potentially ambiguous, and the semantic relationship between the clauses is paraphrase, repetition, amplification, opposition, addition, or summary.
> 3. Style—the usage level is General English or Informal English.
> 4. Rhetorical—the effect is rapidity of movement and/or emphasis.[43]

I think that rule is a bit complicated. Not short, not sweet.

You might be thinking it's easy to criticize a rule and wonder whether I can come up with a more clearly defined rule. And yes, I can. My rule is this: As for when comma splices might be acceptable, "I know it when I see it."[44] Another rule of thumb that best-selling author, Lynne Truss,

---

40. STRUNK & WHITE, *supra* note 19, at 6–7.

41. *Id.*

42. Brosnahan, *supra* note 16, at 184.

43. *Id.* at 185.

44. "I know it when I see it" is an expression used to categorize an observable fact or event, although the category is subjective or lacks clearly defined parameters. Justice Potter Stewart used it in 1964 to describe the threshold test for obscenity in Jacobellis v. Ohio, 378 U.S. 184, 197 (1974) (Stewart, J., concurring).

suggested is, "only do it if you're famous."[45] In fact, her summation of when to use comma splices and when not to is fitting: "Done knowingly by an established writer, the comma splice is effective, poetic, dashing. Done equally knowingly by people who are not published writers, it can look weak or presumptuous. Done ignorantly by ignorant people, it is awful."[46]

I agree. In formal legal writing, avoid comma splices. There are many strategies for fixing a sentence containing a comma splice, so use one of them, and fix the problem.

45. LYNNE TRUSS, EATS, SHOOTS & LEAVES 88 (Gotham Books 2004).
46. *Id.*

"I get the feeling he thinks he's better than us."

3

Semicolons Are Like Kale

Some Writers Like Them and Some Don't, But They Are Good for You If You Know How to Use Them

I have a confession to make; I do not like semicolons *or* kale.[1] Please don't judge. In fact, the need to get my feelings about the semicolon off my chest once led me to confess this sin publicly.[2] The pushback I received was spirited and robust. Readers wrote letters to the editor disagreeing with my viewpoint,[3] and two lawyers later wrote another lengthy article titled "Why the World Needs Semicolons" also disagreeing with me.[4] When it comes to semicolons, lawyers get very riled up.

My negative views about semicolons probably stem from many deep-seated psychological issues in my upbringing, but they also stem from seeing my students consistently struggle when using semicolons in their legal writing assignments. In general, students fall into three

---

1. Do not judge me for disliking kale. In September of 2019, in an article in *The Atlantic*, Amanda Mull claims that Americans never really liked kale, and the public's fascination with kale is coming to an end. Amanda Mull, *The Saddest Leafy Green*, ATLANTIC (Sept. 30, 2019), https://www.theatlantic.com/health/archive/2019/09/why-kale/599041/.

2. Diana Simon, *True Confessions of a Legal Writing Professor: Semicolons Suck*, ARIZ. ATT'Y, Apr. 2021, at 20–24. Some of the information contained in this chapter is taken from my article or the robust response to it in the same magazine a few months later. *See* Elizabeth Bingert & Jeffrey Sparks, *Why the World Needs Semicolons*, ARIZ. ATT'Y, Oct. 2021, at 12–16.

3. *E.g.*, Stephen W. Baum, Letter to the Editor, *Semicolons Seal the Deal*, ARIZ. ATT'Y, Jan. 2022, at 8.

4. Bingert & Sparks, *supra* note 2.

camps: they never use them,[5] they use them everywhere (and frequently improperly),[6] or they use them carefully, consciously, and correctly. I am fairly certain that the smallest subset of students is those who use them correctly.

This chapter will trace the story of the semicolon, the opposing views about them, their significance in court decisions, and finally, what you really want to know—when to use them, when not to use them, and how to use them properly.

Before we get into those topics, though, while everyone knows what a semicolon looks like, most of us have not really thought much about its function. Perhaps unlike any other punctuation mark, writers have given the semicolon nicknames, and those names are helpful in thinking about when to use them. For example, legal writing expert Bryan Garner has referred to it as the "king comma" because it is often used where the writer believes a stronger break in a sentence is needed, and a comma will not do.[7] It has also been called "the great mediator" in situations where a period might be too strong, but a comma might be too weak.[8] At other times, it has been called a "soft period."[9] In her best-selling book *Eats, Shoots & Leaves,* British author Lynne Truss calls it a "compliment from the writer to the reader."[10] Why is it a compliment? Because the writer is saying to the reader "I trust you to see the connection between the parts of this sentence. I do not need to spell it out for you."[11] For his part, author Kurt Vonnegut spelled out his thoughts

---

5. I am not alone in experiencing this. *See* Anne Enquist, *The Semicolon's Undeserved Mystique,* 12 Persp.: Teaching Legal Rsch. & Writing 105, 105 (2004) (noting that one of her students mentioned that she never used semicolons); Suzanne E. Rowe, *Increasing Value in Your Writing Portfolio,* Or. St. Bar Bull., June 2019, at 15, 15 ("faint-hearted [writers] are inclined to simply avoid them altogether.").

6. Legal writing expert Suzanne Rowe has made this same observation. Rowe, *supra* note 5, at 15 ("Few writers know how to use them correctly….").

7. Bryan A. Garner, The Redbook: A Manual on Legal Style 15 (4th ed. 2018) [hereinafter Redbook].

8. Kelley Lonergan, *The Semicolon: A Love Story,* Thought Catalog (Feb. 18, 2014), https://thoughtcatalog.com/kelley-lonergan/2014/02/the-semicolon-a-love-story/

9. Enquist, *supra* note 5, at 105.

10. Lynne Truss, Eats, Shoots & Leaves 124 (Gotham Books 2004).

11. *Id.* at 124–25. This thinking, however, is one reason the semicolon and I part ways. If it takes too much time to find the connection between two ideas, or there is no

on the semicolon bluntly, saying, "When Hemingway killed himself, he put a period at the end of his life. Old age is more like a semicolon."[12] And Cecelia Watson, who filled an entire book with information about the semicolon, has referred to it as a "chimera" with its "colon head and comma tail."[13] I think of it as the yellow light of punctuation because it says, slow down, but don't stop.[14] It is a hybrid—a cross between a comma and a colon.

Therefore, if you suddenly find yourself as a contestant on *Jeopardy!*, and the answer is a cross between a comma and a colon, it is stronger than a comma and weaker than a period, now you know the question: what is the semicolon? (And I expect you to share your winnings with me.)

A. A Divisive Symbol

The semicolon has been in use for more than 500 years, so it has longevity.[15] Aldus Manutius, an Italian printer, first invented and used it in 1494. He became the most prominent printer of the Renaissance, and he helped standardize punctuation. The semicolon was first used in a book which Manutius printed giving an account of someone climbing Mt. Etna.

---

connection between the two parts of the sentence despite the writer's belief that there is, then busy readers may get annoyed. *See* Laura Mondragón, *Confessions of a Semicolon Snob*, WRITING. COOP. (Aug. 27, 2019), https://writingcooperative.com/confessions-of-a-semicolon-snob-47c214422963 (quoting founding editor of Slate who believes the semicolon is commonly abused by implying "a relationship between two statements without having to make clear what that relationship is.")

12. Sam Roberts, *Celebrating the Semicolon in a Most Unlikely Location*, N.Y. TIMES (Feb. 18, 2008), https://www.nytimes.com/2008/02/18/nyregion/18semicolon.html.

13. Cecelia Watson, *Nine Things You Didn't Know About the Semicolon*, MILLIONS (July 29, 2019), https://themillions.com/2019/07/9-things-you-didnt-know-about-the-semicolon.html.

14. Author Frank McCourt, who taught English at a high school in New York, described the semicolon as the yellow traffic light of a "New York sentence." Roberts, *supra* note 12. Because I am from Kansas City, Missouri, where people speak at a normal pace, my idea was not inspired by speech patterns of New Yorkers.

15. Melissa Gouty, *The Fascinating History of the Controversial Semicolon*, WRITING COOP. (Jan. 17, 2020), https://writingcooperative.com/the-fascinating-history-of-the-controversial-semicolon-c13918316df2.

Throughout its history, the use of the semicolon has been contro-versial;[16] it has been labeled "the most divisive punctuation mark of the modern era."[17] In fact, in 1837, two law professors in Paris had a duel over whether to use semicolons or not.[18] Yes, an actual duel. Because the professor who thought the semicolon should be used lost, it is too bad the result of that duel is not binding today. Besides sparking violence, the semicolon has been poisonous. In his 1906 novel, author Maarten Maartens wrote about a scientist who developed a special variety of the comma called "*Semicolon Bacillus,* with which he manages to kill several lab rabbits."[19]

Because I do not like semicolons, while I will present both sides, I will lead with the arguments against semicolons (as I would expect all competent lawyers to do). My main objection to the semicolon is that it is overly formal and elitist. Even the semicolon's defenders acknowledge that it has this unsavory reputation.[20] As one *New York Times* article put it, "the semicolon has been largely jettisoned as a pretentious anachro-nism."[21] In fact, when semicolons have been used by people who are not considered "well educated," it has created a stir. For example, in 1977, the New York Police Department speculated that the Son of Sam killer could be a freelance journalist (in other words, well educated) because of his use of a semicolon in his taunting letters.[22] Later, columnist Jimmy Breslin commented that "Berkowitz is the only murderer I ever heard of who knew how to use a semicolon."[23] And more recently, in 2008, when a semicolon appeared on a poster imploring New York City subway rid-

---

16. Wayne Glausser, *What Do Semicolons Mean?*, 53 STYLE 308, 308 (2019), http://www.jstor.org/stable/10.5235/style.53.3fm ("It is a mark of greatness, yet constantly in peril.").

17. Sydney Wertheim & Meghna Chakrabarti, *The History of the Semicolon (and . . . How to Use It)*, WBUR: ON POINT (Aug. 21, 2019), http://www.wbur.org/onpoint/2019/08/21/semicolon-cecelia-watson.

18. Gouty, *supra* note 15.

19. Watson, *supra* note 13.

20. Paul Collins, Has Modern Life Killed the Semicolon? SLATE (June 20, 2008, 4:51 PM), https://slate.com/culture/2008/06/has-modern-life-killed-the-semicolon.html.

21. Roberts, *supra* note 12.

22. Collins, *supra* note 20.

23. *Id.*

ers not to leave their newspapers behind, people were so shocked that the *New York Times* ended up writing an article about the poster and its author because the author, who worked in the transit agency's marketing and service department, was a college graduate who had majored in English and had a master's degree in creative writing.[24] The poster said: "Please put it in a trash can; that's good news for everyone."[25] (By the way, this is a correct use of the semicolon.)

Further proving the point that semicolons are elitist, data journalist Ben Blatt conducted an analysis for *Slate* of the use of semicolons by authors revered for being literary (or "pretentious") versus authors who are considered hugely popular with the masses (and less pretentious). According to the analysis, semicolon use among the more popular authors was much lower (under 75 semicolons per 100,000 words) than use among the more "literary" authors (over 300 semicolons per 100,000 words).[26] In an honest world, if you looked up semicolons in the dictionary, you would find this definition: "elitist punctuation mark; it is full of itself."

Well-known writers agree that the semicolon is overrated. In 1848, Edgar Allan Poe declared he was "mortified" by printers using too many semicolons.[27] Over a century later, Kurt Vonnegut was also against them, stating, "Here is a lesson in creative writing. First rule: Do not use semicolons."[28] Novelists George Orwell and Donald Barthelme also disliked them.[29] Barthelme said this about semicolons: "Why do I avoid, as much as possible, using the semicolon? It is ugly, ugly as a tick on a dog's belly.

---

24. Roberts, *supra* note 12.

25. *Id.*

26. Ben Blatt, *Do Semicolons Make You Pretentious?*, SLATE (May 3, 2017, 8:03 AM), https://slate.com/culture/2017/05/does-using-more-semicolons-make-an-author-more pretentious.html. Examples of "literary" authors considered are Salman Rushdie and John Updike. Examples of "mass market" authors are David Baldacci and James Patterson.

27. Collins, *supra* note 20.

28. KURT VONNEGUT, A MAN WITHOUT A COUNTRY 23 (Random House Trade Paperbacks 2007).

29. Oliver Duff, *Is the Semicolon the Most Hated Punctuation Mark?*, (JULY 25, 2019, 7:05 PM), https://inews.co.uk/opinion/semicolon-most-hated-punctuation-mark-cecelia -watson-318618.

I pinch them out of my prose."[30] A writer on language for the *Los Angeles Times* agreed, declaring that semicolons are favored "by writers who are so proud they know how to use semicolons that they'll happily short-change readers to show off their knowledge."[31] And *Slate's* founding editor, Michael Kinsley, former vice president of the *Harvard Crimson* and a Harvard law school graduate, told the *Financial Times* the semicolon was commonly abused by implying "a relationship between two statements without having to make clear what that relationship is."[32] It is not just writers that have this view. Almost 800,000 people in 2018 shared a web comic that labeled the semicolon "the most feared punctuation mark on earth."[33]

Perhaps it is for these reasons that semicolon usage has declined over time. A 1995 study tallying punctuation in books found a precipitous decline in semicolon usage between the eighteenth and nineteenth centuries, from 68.1 semicolons per thousand words to just 17.7.[34] In another, more recent study, Lancaster University linguists found that semicolon use in British fiction has fallen by 25% over the last 30 years.[35] The researchers suggested that the end of the semicolon is partly a reflection of uncertainty over "how best to use it," and partly the result of deliberate stylistic choices.

There is another side to the story, however, and many writers (including legal writing experts and grammarians) would argue that semicolons are the best invention ever, beating out the printing press, electric light, and the automobile (I am using hyperbole here). Author Lynne Truss writes about the semicolon "waltz[ing] in," a "glamorous" punctuation

---

30. *The Semicolon Is Ugly*, Advice to Writers: Quote of the Day (July 1, 2010), https://advicetowriters.com/advice/2010/7/1/the-semicolon-is-ugly.html#commenting.

31. Duff, *supra* note 29.

32. Trevor Butterworth, *Pause Celebre*, Financial Times (Sept. 16, 2005. https://www.ft.com/content/0ca549d2-25a9-11da-a4a7-00000e2511c8.

33. Duff, *supra* note 29.

34. Wertheim & Chakrabarti, *supra* note 17.

35. Peter Chappell & Ademola Bello, *Short Sentences in Modern Fiction Reflect Social Media Writing Style*, The Times (Nov. 23, 2021, 12:01 AM GMT), https://www.thetimes.co.uk/article/short-sentences-in-modern-fiction-reflect-social-media-writing-style-nqq85rppv.

mark "twirling in the lights from the glitter-ball."[36] She "swoons" when she sees it.[37] Another writer, fond of semicolons, writes that it is "almost always a greater pleasure to come across a semicolon than a period. The period tells you that that is that;... and now you have to move along. But with a semicolon there you get a pleasant little feeling of expectancy; there is more to come; to read on; it will get clearer."[38] He adds, referring to T.S. Eliot's poetry, that what he loves best are the semicolons: "Sometimes you get a glimpse of a semicolon coming, a few lines farther on, and it is like climbing a steep path through woods and seeing a wooden bench just at a bend in the road ahead, a place where you can expect to sit for a moment, catching your breath."[39] In an article entitled, "The Semicolon: A Love Story," the author, as if talking about a passionate love affair (only read on if you are over 17), writes that the ambiguity of the mark "lends to mystery," and "is sexy."[40] Even Abraham Lincoln expressed his fondness for the semicolon (albeit in wording more appropriate for the general audience) stating that "I must say that I have a great respect for the semi-colon; it's a very useful little chap."[41]

Many grammarians also agree that the semicolon is a desirable mark. For example, *Dreyer's English* gives an example of a paragraph consisting of three sentences joined by three semicolons, noting that although the sentences could have been separated by periods instead, that would have resulted in a collection of "plain old sentences" instead of a "paragraph that grabs you by the hand and marches you from beginning to end."[42] Lynne Truss admits her addiction to them in *Eats, Shoots & Leaves*,[43] and *Grammar Girl* applauds them for adding variety to sentence structure.[44] Finally, Strunk & White provides three forms of the same sentence (one

---

36. Truss, *supra* note 10, at 105.

37. *Id*. at 111.

38. Lewis Thomas, *Notes on Punctuation, in* The Medusa and the Snail 125, 126 (1979).

39. *Id*. at 129.

40. Lonergan, *supra* note 8.

41. Watson, *supra* note 13.

42. Benjamin Dreyer, Dreyer's English 44-45 (2019).

43. *See* Truss, *supra* note 10, at 114-15.

44. *See* Mignon Fogarty, Grammar Girl's Quick and Dirty Tips for Better Writing 91 (2008).

with a semicolon, one with a period, and one with a comma) and emphasizes the advantage of using a semicolon over a period or a comma.[45]

Because legal writing experts can have their own preferences in punctuation that may or may not track general style guides, I should disclose that many of these experts (except for me, of course) are dedicated to the survival of the semicolon.

Expert Bryan Garner has described it as a "versatile device in a skillful writer's hand" that has a powerful impact on the reader.[46] Expert Wayne Schiess also rejected the idea that semicolons are useless, because they can do things that make periods and commas look "inept."[47] And expert Suzanne Rowe has compared the semicolon to a lucrative investment—one that can add value to your writing portfolio because of its unique function.[48]

B. The Power of the Semicolon

One shining example of the power of semicolons that both legal and non-legal writing experts like to use is a long sentence from Martin Luther King, Jr.'s "Letter from a Birmingham Jail."[49] In it, King describes the racism he has been subjected to, one horrific instance after another horrific instance, using the semicolon to keep the reader on edge, waiting for the next instance:

---

45. WILLIAM STRUNK, JR. & E. B. WHITE, THE ELEMENTS OF STYLE 6 (4th ed., Longman 1999).

46. REDBOOK, *supra* note 7, at 15.

47. Wayne Schiess, UNIV. TEX. AUSTIN BLOG SERV.: LEGIBLE, *Semicolons: Not So Useless* (Nov. 4, 2014) https://sites.utexas.edu/legalwriting/2014/11/04/semicolons-not-so-useless/.

48. Rowe, *supra* note 5, at 15.

49. MARTIN LUTHER KING, JR., LETTER FROM BIRMINGHAM JAIL [X] (Penguin Classics 2018). *See* Mary Norris, *Sympathy for the Semicolon*, NEW YORKER (July 15, 2019), https://www.newyorker.com/culture/comma-queen/sympathy-for-the-semicolon (discussing Cecelia Watson's use of this quotation to illustrate the power of semicolons); Bingert & Sparks, *supra* note 2, at 14 (using the quotation from the Letter of Birmingham Jail to illustrate the power of semicolons). We also use this letter in our legal writing classes to introduce persuasive writing because it is an excellent example of incorporating logos, pathos, and ethos to persuade your reader.

I guess it is easy for those who have never felt the stinging darts of segregation to say "wait." But when you have seen vicious mobs lynch your mothers and fathers at will and drown your sisters and brothers at whim; when you have seen hate-filled policemen curse, kick, brutalize, and even kill your black brothers and sisters with impunity; when you see the vast majority of your twenty million Negro brothers smothering in an airtight cage of poverty in the midst of an affluent society; when you suddenly find your tongue twisted and your speech stammering as you seek to explain to your six-year-old daughter why she cannot go to the public amusement park that has just been advertised on television, and see tears welling up in her little eyes when she is told that Funtown is closed to colored children, and see the depressing clouds of inferiority begin to form in her little mental sky, and see her begin to distort her little personality by unconsciously developing a bitterness toward white people; when you have to concoct an answer for a five-year-old son asking in agonizing pathos, "Daddy, why do white people treat colored people so mean?"; when you take a cross-country drive and find it necessary to sleep night after night in the uncomfortable corners of your automobile because no motel will accept you; when you are humiliated day in and day out by nagging signs reading "white" and "colored"; when your first name becomes "n[*****]" and your middle name becomes "boy" (however old you are) and your last name becomes "John," and when your wife and mother are never given the respected title "Mrs."; when you are harried by day and haunted by night by the fact that you are a Negro, living constantly at tiptoe stance, never knowing what to expect next, and plagued with inner fears and outer resentments; when you are forever fighting a degenerating sense of "nobodyness"—then you will understand why we find it difficult to wait.[50]

---

50. KING, *supra* note 50, at [X].

In this passage, with each semicolon, the reader "feels increasingly stifled and suffocated, begging for a release from the seemingly endless list of offenses, slights, and atrocities."[51] The semicolons hold "the reader in suspense, waiting, along with King, for justice."[52] While this letter is about much more than its semicolon usage, it is a prime example of the thrilling sort of rhythm semicolons can create.

Love them or hate them, semicolons are not just another punctuation mark; they have been the focus of many disputes and impacted the lives of many. For example, a city charter had this rule about whether a mayor could demote or suspend officers and employees:

> [the mayor] shall have authority, subject to confirmation by the board, to make appointments, promotions and transfers of employees; to make demotions, suspensions and removals of officers and employees for cause; and may delegate such authority as he deems advisable.[53]

An issue arose as to whether the mayor could demote, suspend, or remove an officer or employee without obtaining approval of the board (or the city council). The resolution of the issue boiled down to the semicolon after the word "employees." Did the first clause requiring confirmation of the board apply to the second clause referring to demotions, suspensions, and removals? The conclusion was that it did not. The second clause said nothing about requiring confirmation of the board. Finding that "the argument that semicolons are not meant to be semicolons [did] violence... to the rules of grammar concerning semicolons," the conclusion was that the punctuation was deliberate, and the use of the semicolon meant that each clause, because it was separated by a semicolon, was independent.[54]

---

51. Bingert & Sparks, *supra* note 2, at 14.

52. Norris, *supra* note 50.

53. Sidney D. Hemsley, Mun. Tech. Advisory Serv., Univ. of Tenn., Use of the Semicolon Under Rules of Statutory Construction 1 (updated 2017) (2005), https://www.mtas.tennessee.edu/system/files/knowledgebase/original/Use%20of%20Semi -Colon%20public_rev2017.pdf.

54. *Id.* at 1–2.

The meaning of a semicolon that Congress used in passing an immigration law also generated disputes revolving around how much time the government had to deport a non-citizen of the United States for commission of a crime.[55] The key part of the statute in question authorized the Secretary of Labor to deport certain classes of non-citizens as follows:

> At any time within five years after entry, any alien who at the time of entry was a member of one or more classes excluded by law;... any alien who was convicted, or who admits the commission, prior to entry, of a felony or other crime or misdemeanor involving moral turpitude;....[56]

In *Pillisz v. Smith*, a citizen of Hungary had been convicted of manslaughter before entering the United States. Seven years after he had been admitted into the country, the Secretary of Labor instituted proceedings to deport him for committing this crime prior to entry. The Hungarian citizen admitted that he had committed manslaughter but argued that the government had to institute proceedings to deport him within five years of his entry into the United States, and so the proceedings were instituted too late. The issue thus was whether the five-year limitation applied to all parts of the statute or only the parts before the semicolon. Relying on the use of the semicolon, the court held that the five-year limitation did not apply to crimes committed before entry because the semicolon was "used to separate the various classes subject to deportation." Because "the semicolon is used to separate a completed thought in one clause from other related matter in another clause of the sentence," the court concluded that Congress intended to define different classes of non-citizens but provided that certain classes could be taken into custody and deported at any time.[57]

Similarly, the Ninth Circuit relied upon this same semicolon to hold that a British citizen could be deported more than five years after enter-

---

55. *E.g.*, Pillisz v. Smith, 46 F.2d 769 (9th Cir. 1931) (construing 8 U.S.C. § 155 (1926) (repealed 1952)); McLeod v. Nagle, 48 F.2d 189 (9th Cir. 1931) (same).

56. *Pillisz*, 46 F.2d at 770 (quoting 8 U.S.C. § 155 (1926)). The full text of the statute is quite lengthy, so only the pertinent portions have been included even though the court did evaluate the entire statute in interpreting it.

57. *Id.* at 771.

ing the United States when he was convicted of breaking and entering before that entry.[58] Relying on both the Oxford and Crowell dictionaries and their definitions of a semicolon, the court explained that the "semicolon effectually isolates the opening clause and its dependent phrase from the other and subsequent clauses."[59] Thus, the court held that the British citizen could be deported even though proceedings were instituted more than five years after entry.

Semicolons have been the focal point of decisions involving many other statutes, such as the extent of benefits an injured worker is entitled to under state law[60] and the scope of the law involving illegal possession of a firearm under federal law.[61] In the case involving the state workers' compensation statute, the court had this to say about the use of semicolons and how they differ from commas: "A semicolon is used to show 'a stronger separation between the parts of a sentence than does a comma.' ... It is used to 'separate phrases, clauses, or enumerations, of almost equal importance, especially when such phrases or clauses contain commas within themselves.'"[62]

A federal district court made this same point about a semicolon used in a federal statute prohibiting possession of a firearm, noting that because the statute closed the words not with a comma, but with a semicolon, the clause in question represented a "completed thought, rather than a pause in an enumeration of related ideas."[63]

Accordingly, semicolons are not just a mark that you can figure out how to use and then forget about; whether semicolons or commas are used can control the meaning of a law and the outcome of a court decision.[64]

---

58. *McLeod*, 48 F.2d at 190–91.

59. *Id.* at 191.

60. State v. Slaugh, 312 P.3d 676, 677–78 (Wash. Ct. App. 2013).

61. United States v. Coward, 151 F. Supp. 2d 544, 545, 548 (E.D. Pa. 2001).

62. *Slaugh*, 312 P.3d at 680 (first quoting MADELINE SEMMELMEYER & DONALD O. BOLANDER, THE NEW WEBSTER'S GRAMMAR GUIDE 235 (BERKELY ED. 1991); and then quoting LOIS IRENE HUTCHINSON, STANDARD HANDBOOK FOR SECRETARIES 239 (8th ed. 1979)).

63. *Coward*, 151 F. Supp. at 548.

64. Interestingly, the presence of a semicolon created an international firestorm after World War II. The issue had to do with the definition of crimes against humanity, and the

C. When to Use Semicolons — and
When to Avoid Them

Now you know that semicolons have supporters and detractors, and you understand how they can impact not just the quality of your writing but the outcome of a case. It is now time to turn to the rules on when to use them and when not to use them.

One place you will often want to use semicolons is when you recite a lengthy list of items in a series, either where there is an internal comma or if semicolons would make the sentence clearer.[65] This often happens in legal writing because legal tests tend to be long and consist of several elements. For example, some courts use a multi-factor test to determine whether an attorney owes a duty to someone who is not a client (yes, this duty can arise). The six factors are:

> (1) the extent to which the transaction was intended to affect the plaintiff; (2) the foreseeability of harm to the plaintiff; (3) the degree of certainty that the plaintiff suffered injury; (4) the closeness of the connection between the defendant's conduct and the injury; (5) the policy of preventing future harm; and (6) the extent to which the profession would be unduly burdened by a finding of liability.[66]

Because some of these items are long, it improves clarity if semicolons are used instead of commas.[67]

This would also be the case if internal commas are used within each element. Here is an example of such a list:

---

result was that a semicolon used in an international law was amended to include a comma instead. *See, e.g.,* Sean O'Reilly, *How a Semicolon Changed International Law,* MEDIUM (July 20, 2018), https://medium.com/@sean.patrick.oreilly96/how-a-semicolon-changed -international-law-292f012bc813; Protocol Rectifying Discrepancy in the Text of Charter, *in* 22 THE TRIAL OF GERMAN MAJOR WAR CRIMINALS 556 (1950), https://heinonline. org/HOL/P?h=hein.trials/trlgmwcr0022&i=568.

65. REDBOOK, *supra* note 7, at 17.

66. Trask v. Butler, 872 P.3d 1080, 1083 (Wash. 1994) (internal citation omitted); *see* Goldberg v. Frye, 266 Cal. Rptr. 483, 489 (Ct. App. 1990) (internal citation omitted).

67. *See* Enquist, *supra* note 5, at 106; REDBOOK, *supra* note 7, at 17.

To evaluate the best interest of the child in connection with a requested name change, we consider six nonexclusive factors:

(1) the name that would best avoid anxiety, embarrassment, inconvenience, confusion, or disruption for the child, which may include consideration of parental misconduct and the degree of community respect (or disrespect) associated with the name;

(2) the name that would best help the child's associational identity within a family unit, which may include whether a change in name would positively or negatively affect the bond between the child and either parent or the parents' families;

(3) assurances by the parent whose last name the child will bear that the parent will not change his or her surname at a later time;

(4) the length of time the child has used one surname and the level of identity the child has with the surname;

(5) the child's preference, along with the age and maturity of the child; and

(6) whether either parent is motivated by concerns other than the child's best interest—for example, an attempt to alienate the child from the other parent.[68]

This usage of semicolons is not limited to legal tests; they also can occur in contracts, as shown by this example:

All other details as to format, title, time, and manner of production; price, publication, and advertisement; and the number and distribution of editorial-review and free copies will be left to the Publisher's discretion.[69]

Another common place to use semicolons is between *two independent clauses* (an independent clause is a group of words that contains a

---

68. Anderson v. Dainard, 478 S.W. 3d 147, 151 (Tex. App. 2015) (internal citation omitted).

69. Schiess, *supra* note 48.

subject and verb and expresses a complete thought) *not joined by a conjunction* if the two clauses are related to each other.[70] Here is an example:

She is 40 and living at home; her father still does her laundry.

Although these two clauses could stand alone as separate sentences with a period after each one, they are connected, and the semicolon signals that relationship better than a period after the first clause. If you are thinking, well, you could use a comma between those two clauses, you would be wrong because that would be an improper comma splice.[71]

Another suitable time to use a semicolon is when the first clause is an independent clause, and the second clause begins with a transitional word or phrase rather than a conjunction.[72] Take this example:

The student was supposed to turn his motion in on Friday at 5:00 p.m.; however, he had stayed up late studying the night before, so he was sound asleep at 5:00 and missed the deadline.

Again, although you could use a period after "p.m." to create two sentences, because the two ideas are related, a semicolon better shows this relationship. A comma cannot be used in this example because that would result in a run-on sentence.[73]

You are probably thinking that these rules seem so easy that no lawyer could bungle them. But lawyers do. Gerald Lebovits, a longtime New York City judge, and a prolific author on matters of legal writing and practice, has created a list of the most common errors he has seen law-

---

70. REDBOOK, *supra* note 7, at 15.

71. *See* Chapter 2 on comma splices.

72. REDBOOK, *supra* note 7, at 16.

73. *See* Chapter 2 on comma splices. *See also* Rowe, *supra* note 5, at 16-17 (noting that to join two sentences with an adverb like however, moreover, etc. you need a semicolon before the adverb and a comma afterward, and while many writers and some publications now use a simple comma before the adverb, they "are wrong." Another occasion to use a semicolon instead of a comma is when you have independent clauses connected by a coordinating conjunction, such as and, but, or, for, so, or yet. The semicolon can be used to help the reader better understand a complex sentence or to indicate a longer break than a comma would suggest. Garner provides this example:

"Courts relying on legislative history often make no pretense that they have developed and are using a theory derived from it; and history often seems to be used only when it supports a conclusion arrived at by other means." REDBOOK, *supra* note 7, at 16.

yers make, so use this checklist when you are scouring your writing for errors on semicolon usage:[74]

Do not use a comma when the situation calls for a semicolon. Semicolons are used to join two independent clauses not joined by a conjunction. If you use a comma instead, that would be an improper comma splice.

Do not use a semicolon when the situation calls for a comma. Take this example: Although he usually walks his dog on a leash; today, he forgot the leash. That semicolon needs to be a comma because the first part of the clause is not an independent clause.

Do not mix up colons with semicolons. A colon introduces elements that illustrate the information preceded by the colon, while a semicolon connects two closely related independent clauses. Judge Lebovits provides this example: "there are two parties in a lease agreement: lessor and lessee."[75] If you changed the colon to a semicolon, that would be incorrect.

Do not use a semicolon when the ideas are not closely related to each other. For example: It was cold outside; I fed my dog kibble bits. These main clauses are not related to each other, so a semicolon would only result in confusion because the reader would not be able to see a relationship between these ideas.[76] On the other hand, "My dog was hungry; I fed her kibble bits," would be a proper use of a semicolon.

In addition to these common mistakes, if you substitute a dash for a semicolon, keep in mind that a dash is more informal than a semicolon, and it has been suggested that a dash is more appropriate than a semicolon only when the relationship between the two clauses is more attenuated and indirect.[77]

The final mistake that many people make (including many of my own students) is making the wrong decision about whether to use a comma or a semicolon with a transitional phrase, such as "however." Do not assume every however needs a semicolon before it. A good rule of

---

74. Gerald Lebovits, *The Worst Mistakes in Legal Writing—Part II*, N.Y. St. Bar Ass'n J., March/April 2018, at 62-64.

75. *Id.* at 62.

76. Fogarty, *supra* note 45, at 91.

77. Truss, *supra* note 10, at 122-23.

thumb is to see if you can read a complete sentence if you take out the "however." If you can, then you only need a comma.[78] Here are examples of where you use a semicolon and where you do not:

> Need a semicolon and cannot use a comma: She went with her daughter to buy groceries; however, when they arrived, the store was closed.

> Need a comma and cannot use a semicolon: They walked to the grocery store, however, even though it was seven miles away.

Do not be like me—a semicolon hater. Lean into the semicolon because it will, if used correctly, spice up your writing; sometimes, a comma, a colon, a period, or a dash just will not do.

---

78. Rowe, *supra* note 5, at 17.

"Your honor, in my defense, he didn't use a serial comma."

It Has Ruined Lives, Polarized People, and Cost Companies Millions of Dollars
Say Hello to the Serial Comma

How could a punctuation mark ruin someone's life? Well, for example, it could if a dispute between style manuals turned violent, and an innocent passerby got in the middle and died of a gunshot wound.[1] Fortunately, this news was published in *The Onion*, a satirical publication, so it is not true. But it is true that the *New York Times* has referred to the serial comma as "perhaps the most polarizing of punctuation marks."[2] It is also true that in the British bestseller, *Eats, Shoots & Leaves*, the author explains that some people embrace the serial comma, and some people do not, but "*never* get between these people when drink has been taken."[3] And be prepared to learn that the absence of a serial comma could cost you, or your client, millions of dollars.

In case you do not know what a serial comma is, it is a comma placed immediately after the next to the last term where "and" or "or" are used in a series of three or more terms. For example, if you say my favorite desserts are brownies, chocolate chip cookies, and chocolate cake,

---

1. *4 Copy Editors Killed in Ongoing AP Style, Chicago Manual Gang Violence*, The Onion (Jan. 7, 2013, 9:50 AM), https://www.theonion.com/4-copy-editors-killed-in-ongoing-ap-style-chicago-man-1819574341.

2. Daniel Victor, *Lack of Oxford Comma Could Cost Maine Company Millions in Overtime Dispute*, N.Y. Times (March 16, 2017), nytimes.com/2017/03/16/us/oxford-comma-lawsuit.html.

3. Lynne Truss, Eats, Shoots & Leaves 84 (Gotham Books 2004).

the comma after cookies is the serial comma (If you don't like chocolate, I can't help you).

And because all effective legal writers place the conclusion up front, I will do that here: Use serial commas. Please. But saying use them without explaining a lot more about them would be like saying, "There was a Revolutionary War" and stopping there. You would want to know why it started, what happened during it, and who won—little details like that. Accordingly, this chapter will venture beyond the advice to "just use them."

A. Serial, Oxford, or Harvard?

Before we delve into the controversy swirling around serial commas, let's start with what they are called, as they go by several names: serial comma, Oxford comma, Harvard comma, (notice the serial comma there) and series comma. After a survey in which I polled no one, it looks like legal writers prefer the phrase serial comma.[4] But it's not just legal writers that call it that. Strunk & White does, and so does Grammar Girl.[5] The Oxford comma label is also used frequently.

Why is it called the Oxford comma, and who first invented it? It is called the Oxford comma because the Oxford University Press started the movement to use it.[6] When it was first invented, however, is somewhat of a mystery, and you will find when you become a lawyer, delving into minutiae such as who first invented the Oxford comma is considered a fun thing to do during your leisure time. Either it was someone named F. H. Collins, who wrote the *Authors' and Printers' Dictionary* in

---

4. *See* Bryan A. Garner, The Redbook: A Manual on Legal Style 3 (4th ed. 2018) [hereinafter Redbook]; O'Connor v. Oakhurst Dairy, 851 F.3d 69, 75 n.5 (1st Cir. 2017). *But see* Elitza Meyer, *It's Not the Oxford Comma, It's the Ambiguity*, 8 Hous. L. Rev. 25, 25 (2017) (calling it the Oxford comma).

5. William Strunk, Jr. & E. B. White, The Elements of Style 2 (4th ed., Longman 1999); Mignon Fogarty, Grammar Girl's Quick and Dirty Tips for Better Writing 100 (2008).

6. Jasso Lamberg, *Origin of the Oxford Comma*, Comdesres (Feb. 23, 2015), comdesres. com/origin-of-the-oxford-comma; *Why We Do Give a F*** About the Oxford Comma (and Why You Should Too)*, PerfectIt (Aug. 18, 2005), https://intelligentediting.com/blog/why-we-do-give-a-fstarstarstar-about-the-oxford-comma-and-why-you-should-too/.

1905, or it could have been Herbert Spencer, who Collins referenced in his book as the person who recommended using a serial comma,[7] or it was someone named Horace Hart, who wrote *Rules for Compositors and Readers at the University Press Oxford* in 1905. But one thing we know for sure: somebody invented it.

As far as where the "Harvard comma" comes from, that is less clear except that the Harvard University Press style guide recommends it.[8]

The term "series" comma was coined in *Dreyer's English* because the author was of the view that the term "serial comma" conjures up images of serial killers.[9] Notwithstanding Dreyer's view, I would just call it the serial comma as my first choice and Oxford comma as my second choice. Or maybe they are tied for first.

B. Proponents, Opponents, and Fence Sitters

Not surprisingly, the confusion about what to call them is like the confusion surrounding when to use them. There are two schools of thought—use them and do not use them—the kind of dispute lawyers love.

If the people against serial commas sued the people supporting serial commas in court (I'm not sure what the damages would be, but lawyers are surprisingly creative), the sides would be about even. Who is against serial commas? Journalists typically do not like the serial comma because they take up space.[10] For example, the Associated Press, considered the authority in most American newsrooms, recommends against using the serial comma for a simple series.[11] If you are from Britain, the

---

7. Lamberg, *supra* note 6.

8. *Defining, Understanding, and Embracing the Serial Comma*, PRINCETON WRITES, https://pwrites.princeton.edu/tools-and-insights/defining-understanding-and-using-the-serial-comma/ (last visited Jan. 23, 2022).

9. BENJAMIN DREYER, DREYER'S ENGLISH 24–25 (2019).

10. PRINCETON WRITES, *supra* note 8.

11. *Ask the Editor Frequently Asked Style Questions*, ASSOC. PRESS STYLEBOOK, apstylebook.com/ask_the_editor_faq (last visited Jan. 23, 2022).

standard is not to use it, which seems very odd considering its birthplace at the Oxford University Press.[12]

But there are also many people steadfastly in favor of the serial comma, including most importantly for our purposes, legal writing experts. For example, expert Bryan Garner advises to "use the serial comma consistently."[13] Professor Richard C. Wydick also says to use the serial comma.[14] Many other legal writing experts agree.[15]

But it's not just legal writers. In *Dreyer's English*, Dreyer's strongly held view is that "[o]nly godless savages eschew the series comma."[16] Using less vivid wording, the United States Government Publishing Office's Style Manual says to use it,[17] Strunk & White says to use it,[18] *The American Medical Association's Manual of Style* says to use it,[19] and so does *The American Psychological Association Style Guide*.[20]

And then there are the fence sitters. The *Chicago Manual of Style* recommends it but also qualifies this by saying "the serial comma is optional."[21] Lynne Truss, author of *Eats, Shoots & Leaves*, says not to be too rigid about it because "[s]ometimes the sentence is improved by including it; sometimes it isn't."[22]

---

12. Truss, *supra* note 3, at 84.

13. Redbook, *supra* note 4, at 4.

14. Richard C. Wydick, Plain English for Lawyers 92 (4th ed. 1998).

15. Susie Salmon, *To Oxford or Not to Oxford? A Serial (Comma) Dilemma*, Ariz. Att'y, April 2014, at 12 ("an ardent devotee of the serial... comma"); Anne Enquist & Laurel Currie Oats, Just Writing: Grammar Punctuation and Style for the Legal Writer 245 (2d ed. 2005) ("legal writers should make it a habit to include it").

16. Dreyer, *supra* note 9, at 24.

17. U.S. Gov't Publ'g Off., Style Manual 202 (2016), https://www.govinfo.gov/content/pkg/GPO-STYLEMANUAL-2016/pdf/GPO-STYLEMANUAL-2016.pdf.

18. Strunk & White, *supra* note 5, at 2.

19. *See Advice for the AMA Style Newbie*, AMAStyleInsider (Jan. 26, 2018), https://amastyleinsider.com/2018/01/26/advice-ama-style-newbie/.

20. *Serial Comma*, American Psych. Ass'n: APA Style (Sept. 2019), apastyle.apa.org/style-grammar-guidelines/punctuation/serial-comma.

21. *See Commas*, Chi. Manual of Style, https://www.chicagomanualofstyle.org/qanda/data/faq/topics/Commas/faq0066.html (last visited Jan. 23, 2022).

22. Truss, *supra* note 3, at 85.

You are a legal writer, so do not sit on the fence. Instead, adopt the view that it is "never incorrect."[23]

You might be left thinking that people who care about writing care about the serial comma, but the public is not that interested (and you might also find that reading this, you fall into the camp that does not really care even though you know you should). The public was polled on the Oxford comma, however, and they have views. But before I tell you what the result was, take a guess on whether it won or lost.

Take a second. Ready for the answer?

It won but not by much. FiveThirtyEight asked 1,129 Americans what they thought about the Oxford comma.[24] The Oxford comma won—57% in favor and 43% against—but in the article reporting the results, the results were reported as falling "pretty much down the middle."[25] Interestingly, if you are someone who prefers the Oxford comma, this same article says you tend to be the kind of person who thinks your own grammar is excellent—zealous, "but not really the humble type."[26]

Is this just a case of style without any real consequences? Well, no. In some instances, serial commas can make or break a case.

C. For Want of a Comma

In one case, the absence of a serial comma almost resulted in a court dismissing charges leveled against a defendant for animal cruelty when he failed to seek medical care for his sick cat (cat lovers do not wor-

---

23. Redbook, *supra* note 4, at 4.

24. Walt Hicky, *Elitist, Superfluous, or Popular? We Polled Americans on the Oxford Comma,* (Jun. 17, 2014), https://fivethirtyeight.com/features/elitist-superfluous-or-popular-we-polled-americans-on-the-oxford-comma/. Founded by Nate Silver in 2008, FiveThirtyEight is a politics, sports, and science website focusing on data-driven journalism. *FiveThirtyEight,* Wikipedia, https://en.wikipedia.org/wiki/FiveThirtyEight (last visited Jan. 23, 2022); *see also About Us,* FiveThirtyEight, https://fivethirtyeight.com/about-us/ (last visited Jan. 23, 2022).

25. *Id.*

26. *Id.*

ry—the charges ultimately stuck).[27] In *People v. Walsh*,[28] a defendant was charged with laws prohibiting animal cruelty. I will not go into the gory details about the cat's condition, but a veterinarian involved in the case believed that the defendant medically neglected the cat. One key part of the law that defendant was charged with provided, in part, that a person who "deprives any animal of necessary sustenance, food or drink" is guilty of a misdemeanor.[29] The essence of the defendant's argument was that because of the absence of a serial comma after "food," the word "sustenance" only included food or drink and did not include medical care. (Well, the defendant did not word his argument quite that way.) Therefore, he argued, the charges should be dismissed.

Addressing the defendant's argument, the court agreed that if the statute intended to list three types of deprivation, it would have read "sustenance, food, or drink."[30] Noting that three or more items in a series should be separated by commas, the court gave the classic example of an author's dedication in a book that should have used a serial comma but did not: "to my parents, the Pope and Mother Theresa."[31] The absence of a comma after Pope in that phrase, the court stated, indicated that the author's parents were the Pope and Mother Theresa, which is inaccurate. Because the court had to follow the actual wording of the statute, it agreed that the failure to provide an animal with medical care was not included in the phrase "necessary sustenance," and so the defendant could not be guilty of that part of the statute. Fortunately, for the cat, the legislature used many broad and ambiguous words after the sustenance phrase, and the court was able to fit the defendant's conduct within those remaining words.[32] Thus, the court did not dismiss the charges.[33]

---

27. The idea to use this as an example with first-year law students came from Susan J. Hankin, *Statutory Interpretation in the Age of Grammatical Permissiveness: An Object Lesson for Teaching Why Grammar Matters*, 18 PERSPS.: TEACHING LEGAL RSCH. & WRITING 105 (2010).

28. No. 2007NY022001, 2208 WL 724724, at *1 (N.Y. Crim. Ct. Jan. 3, 2008).

29. *Id.*

30. *Id.* at *2.

31. *Id.*

32. *Id.* at *3.

33. *Id.* at *4.

Although the missing serial comma did not absolve the defendant of wrongdoing in *Walsh*, another missing serial comma did end up costing an employer millions of dollars in *O'Connor v. Oakhurst Dairy*.[34] (I told you that I would tell you about it, and now I am.) If you think I am making it up that one comma caused the problem, this is what the court said at the beginning of its opinion: "For want of a comma, we have this case."[35]

This situation was more complicated than the one involving the cat, so pay close attention. This case took place in Maine, where the legislature had passed laws dealing with the paying of wages, the rules for overtime for employees, etc. The law provided "employees" would receive overtime for working more than 40 hours a week, but it excluded certain workers from the definition of employees, who were not entitled to overtime. The law at issue stated that the protection of the overtime law does not apply to:

> The canning, processing, preserving, freezing, drying, marketing, storing, packing for shipment or distribution of:
> (1) Agricultural produce;
> (2) Meat and fish products; and
> (3) Perishable foods.[36]

Enter three truck drivers, who sued their employer for more than four years' worth of overtime pay that their employer had not paid them.[37] The problem was that these delivery drivers *distributed* perishable foods, but they did not *pack* the boxes themselves.[38] In other words, the drivers argued, the words meant that the exempted activity was "packing," whether that packing was for shipment or distribution. And since the drivers did not pack perishable foods, the exemption did not apply to them (hence, they were entitled to overtime). For its part, their employer argued, the words were meant to exempt "packing for shipment" and "distribution" as two separate activities, and since the drivers *did* "dis-

---

34. 851 F.3d 69 (1st Cir. 2017); *see* Victor, *supra* note 2.
35. *Id.* at 70.
36. *Id.* at 71.
37. Victor, *supra* note 2.
38. *O'Connor*, 851 F.3d at 71.

tribute" (i.e., transport) the foods, they were exempt (and no overtime was due).

This all depends on how you interpret the words "packing for shipment or distribution of… perishable foods." If the word "distribution" is modifying packing, then it isn't a separate activity, and the drivers *should* be entitled to overtime pay. However, if the word "distribution" is considered a standalone, exempt activity, then the drivers *would not* be entitled to overtime pay. The point is that because of the missing comma, the meaning was unclear.

Ultimately, for a variety of reasons, including the ambiguity arising from the serial comma's omission, the court ruled in favor of the drivers. In doing so, the court noted the "clarifying virtues of serial commas that other jurisdictions recognized."[39]

In fact, there are examples where laws have included serial commas, and courts have relied upon those commas to find that the comma helped clarify the meaning of the law.[40] For example, in *Sullivan v. Abraham*,[41] the plaintiff sued the defendant for defamation, but the defendant asked the court to dismiss the lawsuit under another law, and it did. Once that happened, another Texas law provided that if there is a dismissal, the prevailing party can recover attorney's fees and other expenses. Accordingly, the defendant requested some $67,000 in attorney's fees and some $4,000 in costs. After a hearing, however, the court announced that "justice and equity" necessitated reducing the defendant's recovery in fees to only $6,500 and costs to only $1,500.[42] Unhappy with these reduced amounts, the defendant appealed. The law in question provided as follows:

> If the court orders dismissal of a legal action under this chapter, the court shall award to the moving party: (1) court costs, reasonable attorney's fees, and other expenses incurred in defend-

---

39. *Id.* at 75, n. 5.

40. *E.g.*, In re ReadyOne Indus., Inc., 394 S.W. 3d 689, 695 (Tex. App. 2012) (finding that the use of a comma before the conjunction clarified the issue, and the use of the serial comma serves to resolve ambiguity); Deal v. Coleman, 751 S.E.2d 337, 341 (Ga. 2013) (finding that the statute could only be interpreted one way because of the serial comma, and its use is the only ironclad method of avoiding unnecessary ambiguities).

41. 488 S.W.3d 294, 295 (Tex. 2016).

42. *Id.* at 295–96.

ing against the legal action as justice and equity may require....[43]

The defendant argued that he should have received all attorneys' fees because the phrase "as justice and equity may require" only modified "other
expenses," and not the phrase "reasonable attorney's fees."[44] Specifically,
the defendant argued that if the legislature had intended for attorney's
fees to be adjusted based on equity and justice, it would have eliminated
the serial comma after attorney's fees.[45] While the court stated that the
presence of the serial comma was "not definitive," it agreed that its use
indicated that the legislature intended to limit the justice-and-equity
modifier to other expenses.[46] Thus, the court held that the defendant
was entitled to all reasonable attorneys' fees.

While I would like to convince you that courts primarily rest their
decisions upon correct punctuation (so you would use correct punctuation), that would not be quite accurate. The truth is that in some cases,
the courts have not attached significance to an omitted serial comma.
For example, in *United States v. Bass*,[47] the statute omitted a serial comma, and in response to the government's argument about the missing
comma, the Supreme Court said as follows:

> [M]any leading grammarians, while sometimes noting that
> commas at the end of series can avoid ambiguity, concede that
> use of such commas is discretionary.... When grammarians
> are divided, and surely where they are cheerfully tolerant, we
> will not attach significance to an omitted comma.[48]

Similarly, the Massachusetts Supreme Court in a case involving a serial comma stated that punctuation would not control its outcome, and
courts will disregard a statute's punctuation if it conflicts with principles
of statutory construction.[49] "In other words," the court stated, "to para-

---

43. *Id.* at 296.
44. *Id.* at 297.
45. *Id.* at 297–98.
46. *Id.* at 299.
47. 404 U.S. 350 (1971), superseded by statute.
48. *Id.* at 519 n.6.
49. Defiore v. American Airlines, Inc., 910 N.E.2d 889, 896 (Mass. 2009).

phrase a statement attributed to Sigmund Freud, sometimes a comma is 'just' a comma."[50]

Regardless, you might be interested in learning that legislatures have manuals instructing them how to draft laws (including the United States House of Representatives),[51] and many of those manuals require the use of the serial comma when setting forth a series of words or phrases. For example, the West Virginia bill drafting manual says that the legislature "now uses the serial or 'Oxford' comma. Within a series of words, phrases, or clauses, include a comma with the item before the conjunction, e.g., men, women, and children."[52] Similarly, the Illinois legislature's drafting manual states that "placing a comma before the conjunction will be clear, but omitting the comma may cause ambiguity. Because clarity is one of the cardinal virtues in drafting statutes, follow the practice of inserting a comma before the conjunction."[53] It even gives an example:

> Potentially ambiguous: Real estate is classified as vacant, residential, farm, commercial and industrial.

> In the example, are there 4 or 5 categories? Is "commercial and industrial" one category, or are "commercial" and "industrial" 2 categories?[54]

Clarity is not only a virtue in drafting statutes: it is an essential ingredient of effective legal writing.[55]

Let's consider another example of how the lack of a serial comma can inject ambiguity into a sentence:

---

50. *Id.* at 896–97.

51. For a general discussion of this topic, see Amy Langenfeld, *Capitol Drafting: Legislative Drafting Manuals in the Law School Classroom*, 22 Persps.: Teaching Legal Rsch. & Writing 141 (2014).

52. House Clerk's Office et al., West Virginia Legislature Bill Drafting Manual 36 (2018), https://www.wvlegislature.gov/legisdocs/misc/pub/Drafting_Manual.pdf.

53. Legislative Reference Bureau, Illinois Bill Drafting Manual 232 (2012), http://www.ilga.gov/commission/lrb/manual.pdf.

54. *Id.*

55. Eric P. Voigt, *Explanatory Parentheticals Can Pack a Persuasive Punch*, 45 McGeorge L. Rev. 269, 272–73 (2013) (noting that federal and state judges are persuaded by clear writing, and experts on legal writing agree).

I am taking contracts, legal writing and research.

How many classes am I taking? Two or three? If you had a serial comma after legal writing, the number would be clear: three. Without the serial comma, it could be two or three. And here is another example of ambiguity without a serial comma:

I have four pounds of flour, six pounds of sugar and chocolate chips.

Does this mean that the sugar and chocolate chips together weigh six pounds? Or does it mean that I have six pounds of sugar and six pounds of chocolate chips for a total of 12 pounds? Again, a serial comma after sugar would clear the issue up.

But sometimes, even when you use a serial comma, the meaning may be unclear, so you might need another device to erase the ambiguity by some other means. For example, take this sentence:

The Jetson family sued their neighbor, a lawyer and a judge.

Now, based on that sentence, how many people did the Jetsons sue? It might be just one person—a neighbor who also happens to be a lawyer and a judge. It might be three people—a neighbor, a lawyer, and a judge. It might be two people—their neighbor, who is a lawyer and someone else, who is a judge. If you include a comma after lawyer, the meaning still is unclear because you don't know if the neighbor is a lawyer or if the "lawyer" is someone else entirely. There are several ways to clear this up, but here are a few:

The Jetson family sued their neighbor, who is a lawyer, and a judge. (Two people)

The Jetson family sued their neighbor (a lawyer) and a judge. (Two people)

The Jetson family sued their neighbor (a lawyer and a judge). (One person).

The Jetson family sued their neighbor, who is both a lawyer and a judge. (One person)

The Jetson family sued their neighbor as well as a lawyer and a judge (Three people).

Also, as much as I hate to admit it, sometimes omitting a serial comma will not impact clarity. For example, take this sentence:

I love hiking, riding bikes and river rafting.

This sentence is clear without the serial comma after bikes.

But remember—because using a serial comma is "never incorrect," use it.

D. Some Serial Commas Are Less Correct Than Others

Are there exceptions to the "always use the serial comma" rule? Of course there are, or I would not have asked that question. There are essentially three. First, if the items in the series are long and complex, or if they contain internal punctuation or a conjunction, separate them with a semicolon instead of a comma.[56] For example, take this sentence:

Every morning, I drink coffee with creamer and sugar; I do my deep breathing exercises; and I walk the dog around the block and make sure he does his business.

Second, there is an exception when the items are all joined by conjunctions.[57] This is called a polysyndeton and just means a repetition of conjunctions in close succession. It is a stylistic device in which several coordinating conjunctions are used in succession to achieve an artistic effect. Polysyndeton examples are found in literature and in day-to-day conversations.

For example, take this sentence from the Wizard of Oz:

Lions and tigers and bears, oh my!

Or the famous creed of the post office:

Neither snow nor rain nor heat nor gloom of night stays these couriers.[58]

---

56. REDBOOK, *supra* note 4, at 4.

57. *Id.*

58. HISTORIAN, U.S. POSTAL SERV., POSTAL SERVICE MISSION AND "MOTTO" 1 (1999), https://about.usps.com/who-we-are/postal-history/mission-motto.pdf.

Finally, when the last element in a series is preceded by an ampersand, you do not use the serial comma.[59] This is an important rule to remember because so many law firms use ampersands in their name. For example, consider the name of this fake law firm:

Lett, Salmon & Simon

No comma should be placed after Salmon.

In conclusion, use the serial comma. Not only is it popular, but it will also help you improve clarity in your writing. Think of me when you do.

---

59. Redbook, *supra* note 4, at 4.

"Your problem is that you're too possessive."

5

The Double Life of the Apostrophe

....

I was breezing along a few years ago thinking that my students under-stood apostrophes. But then I was blindsided. It all happened when I crafted a hypothetical for our first-year students around my favorite series: *Game of Thrones*. Maybe you have heard of it. Anyway, I created a fictional law school named *Westeros* University, and the hypothetical was about *employees* and *employers*, and of course it had a *defendant* and a *plaintiff*. The protagonist? Professor Jaime Lannister. You are probably thinking, what does this have to do with apostrophes? For some reason, when writing many of the words mentioned in the preceding sentence, my students went rogue; they used apostrophes unnecessarily and then forgot apostrophes when they were necessary, as shown in the examples below:

Incorrect Example 1: Summary judgment should be granted in Defendants favor because the book meets the three-factor test under the work-for-hire doctrine.

Incorrect Example 2: In the shadow of Westeros' publishing cul-ture, Lannister wrote the Work, which was applicable to the veteran student population in his classroom.

Incorrect Example 3: Employee's do not need to be solely moti-vated to serve the employer.

Incorrect Example 4: Therefore, an employees work is within the scope of his employment if: "(a) it is of the kind [the em-ployee] is employed to perform; (b) it occurs substantially within the authorized time and space limits; [and] (c) it is actuated, at least in part, by a purpose to serve the [employer]."

Incorrect Example 5: Work is not substantially within the employer's authorized time and space limits when its created during off-hours with employee resources.

Incorrect Example 6: Lannister created the Work because he thought it would improve his class' learning.

Did you spot the problems? Read this chapter; by the end, you should be able to spot the mistakes and correct them.

Please do not judge my students and their apostrophes (or lack thereof). The apostrophe has been dubbed "the most troublesome punctuation mark."[1] The *Oxford Companion to the English Language* agrees that the apostrophe's possessive use is troublesome: "There was never a golden age in which the rules for the use of the possessive apostrophe in English were clear-cut and known, understood, and followed by most educated people."[2]

I think part of the problem is that the apostrophe leads a double life—it serves as a contraction when a letter or letters are omitted from a word, and in entirely different situations, it serves as a possessive—leading to some confusion.[3] The other problem is that people do not always agree on when to use one and when not to, especially when it comes to words ending in *s*.

First, we will trace its history. Second, we will cover the main rules for using apostrophes. Third, we will show you some examples where the placement of an apostrophe has either created ambiguity or a firestorm in legal settings. Finally, we will show you that even the United States Supreme Court cannot agree on when to use one when it comes to the possessive use for words ending in *s*.

---

1. MIGNON FOGARTY, GRAMMAR GIRL'S QUICK AND DIRTY TIPS FOR BETTER WRITING 124 (2008).

2. LYNNE TRUSS, EATS, SHOOTS & LEAVES 39 (Gotham Books 2004) (internal quotation marks and citation omitted); Helene Schumacher, *Have We Murdered the Apostrophe?* BBC (Feb. 23, 2020), https://www.bbc.com/culture/article/20200217-have-we-murdered-the-apostrophe.

3. *See* TRUSS, *supra* note 2, at 43.

A. A Brief History

The apostrophe was probably born in the early sixteenth century.[4] Its birthplace was either Italy or France, and before it became a punctuation mark, it was a rhetorical term used to describe the moment when a speaker would turn from an audience to address an absent person.[5] When apostrophes first were used, they denoted that something had been removed from a word. It was not until the seventeenth or eighteenth century that the mark took on the additional role of the possessive use.

Weirdly, some people are obsessed with either saving the apostrophe or ensuring its correct use. One novelist and columnist for *The Daily Mirror* formed a fictional Association for the Abolition of the Aberrant Apostrophe, where he printed the worst examples of apostrophe mistakes.[6] Similarly, in 2001, a retired editor, John Richards, formed the Apostrophe Protection Society with the goal of preserving the correct use of the apostrophe.[7] Who knew the apostrophe could garner so much attention?

Apostrophes have also sparked litigation and political controversy. But before we get into those topics, let's just cover the basic rules for using the apostrophe, first in *contractions* (where the apostrophe denotes the omission of something), and second, in the *possessive form* (when the apostrophe is going around saying it owns something).

B. Apostrophes and Contractions

Using an apostrophe in a contraction is relatively straightforward. The apostrophe indicates you are either omitting letters or numbers.[8] Here are some examples when the apostrophe substitutes for omitted letters:

---

4. Schumacher, *supra* note 2.

5. *Id.*; *Why Do We Use Apostrophes to Show Possession*, MERRIAM-WEBSTER, https://www.merriam-webster.com/words-at-play/history-and-use-of-the-apostrophe   (last visited Apr. 2, 2022).

6. TRUSS, *supra* note 2, at 47.

7. *Our History*, APOSTROPHE PROT. SOC'Y, https://www.apostrophe.org.uk/history (last visited Apr. 2, 2022); Schumacher, *supra* note 2.

8. BRYAN A. GARNER, THE REDBOOK: A MANUAL ON LEGAL STYLE 59 (4th ed. 2018) [hereinafter REDBOOK]

Original words: She would
Contraction: She'd.

Original words: It is
Contraction: It's

Original words: They are
Contraction: They're.

Original words: Who is
Contraction: Who's

It seems easy, but writers often get confused on whether the word they are using—such as its—is being used as a possessive pronoun or to say, "it is," and I have seen this with my students. Its—without the apostrophe—is a possessive and a pronoun. It's—with the apostrophe—is a contraction standing for "it is."

Let's look at one of the examples from my student's work already quoted above:

> Work is not substantially within the employer's authorized time and space limits when its created during off-hours with employee resources.

Do you see the problem? The word *its* should be *it's* because the meaning is it is, not the possessive use of its.

Here's another student example, where the student included an apostrophe in "its" when one was not called for:

> The court notes that if the crime of burglary is too broadly construed, *it's* effects could essentially terrorize residents.

Because the word *its* is not short for *it is*, the insertion of the apostrophe is incorrect. If you're trying to figure out whether you should write *it's* or *its*, swap in *it is* or *it has*. If the sentence makes sense with either of those substitutions, use *it's*. If the resulting sentence doesn't make sense, you need *its*.

In general, proceed with a bit of caution when using contractions, such as *it's*, *wasn't*, *doesn't*, *won't*, etc., in formal legal writing. While many top legal writing experts believe that using contractions in your writing improves readability and makes your writing more accessible,[9] other experts believe they should be avoided,[10] or used sparingly.[11] For example, Justice Scalia thought that using contractions comes off as an attempt to be "buddy-buddy" with the judge[12] and considered them "an affront to the… court."[13] But when I went searching for contractions in recent Supreme Court opinions, I found a treasure trove of them in a dissenting opinion in a 2019 decision, *Apple Inc. v. Pepper.*[14] In his dissent, Justice Gorsuch, joined by Chief Justice Roberts and Justices Thomas and Alito, used no fewer than 16 individual contractions a total of 26 times, such as "that's," "doesn't," "can't," "we've," "they'll," "there's," and "hadn't."[15] In fact, the dissent used two back-to-back contractions in one sentence as follows: "[T]he Court (re)characterizes *Illinois Brick* as a rule that anyone who purchases goods… can sue, while anyone who doesn't, can't."[16] But the majority not only disagreed with the dissent on the legal issue, it apparently did not even agree on the use of contractions: it did not use a *single* contraction, even when it would have been easy to use contractions as substitutes for word combinations, such as "who is," "there will," "that is," "cannot" "it is," and "there is."[17] Go figure.

---

9. Greg May, *Who Thinks that Contractions ~~Shouldn't~~ Should Not Be Used in Appellate Briefs or Other Legal Writing?*, CAL. BLOG OF APPEAL, https://www.calblogofappeal.com/2008/04/05/who-thinks-that-contractions-shouldnt-should-not-be-used-in-appellate-briefs-or-other-legal-writing/; *see also* REDBOOK, *supra* note 8, at 59 ("Contractions have long been shunned in formal prose. But that taboo is fortunately disappearing.").

10. Gerald Lebovits, *Apostrophe's and Plurals'*, N.Y. ST. BAR ASS'N J., Feb. 2004, at 60, 64 ("Contractions are warm and friendly in informal writing. Contractions aren't appropriate in formal writing."). Note, however, that this article was written in 2004, before attitudes had changed about the use of contractions.

11. May, *supra* note 9.

12. Nina Totenberg, *Justice Scalia: Be Likeable and Avoid Contractions*, NPR (Apr. 28, 2008, 1:00 PM), https://www.npr.org/templates/story/story.php?storyId=90001031.

13. Joel Schumm, *IndyBar: Contractions in Formal Legal Writing: Is It Casual Friday Yet?*, IND. LAW. (Feb. 17, 2021), https://www.theindianalawyer.com/articles/indybar-contractions-in-formal-legal-writing-is-it-casual-friday-yet.

14. 139 S. Ct. 1514 (2019).

15. *Id.* at 1525–31 (Gorsuch, J., dissenting).

16. *Id.* at 1529 (Gorsuch, J., dissenting).

17. *See id.* at 1519–25.

If you are unsure about the use of contractions in formal legal writing, check with your audience—your legal writing professor, your supervisor, or the equivalent.

Let's move on to a different situation, unique to legal writing, where the use of apostrophes can be confusing —the shortened form of case names in citations. Citation guides call for the use of abbreviations for some common case names that are on the longer side, and many of these abbreviations require an apostrophe. For example, if part of a case name uses the word "Society," the *Bluebook* instructs you to shorten that word in the cite to "Soc'y."[18] Similarly, if the case name uses the word "Secretary," that is shortened to "Sec'y."[19] You do not have to wait until casual Friday to use these contractions—no one will ever judge you as being too informal.

Apostrophes are also used to indicate the omission of numerals in a year, such as when you write, "The bill was first introduced in '18."

C. Apostrophes and the Possessive Use

Apostrophes lead a double life. In addition to their use in contractions, they also are used to create possessives. The use of an apostrophe to show a possessive gets more complicated, and there is more disagreement in actual usage, even though, per the *Redbook*, the rules are clear.

1. Use with a Singular Noun That Does Not End in S

Everyone would agree that if you have a singular noun that does not end in *s*, you need an apostrophe *s* ('s) to make the noun possessive. Let's take two words you will use all the time: plaintiff and defendant. If you want to use the possessive for these words, you use an apostrophe *s* like this:

Plaintiff's motion should be denied.
Defendant's complaint should be dismissed.

---

18. The Bluebook: A Uniform System of Citation 307 tbl.T.6, at 307 (Columbia L. Rev. Ass'n et al. eds, 21st ed. 2020).

19. *Id.*

While this seems straightforward, students sometimes conflate a possessive *s* with a plural *s*. Here is an example of a common mistake I see:

> Employee's do not need to be solely motivated to serve the employer.

The word *employee's* [sic] is not being used in the possessive form. It's just a plural noun, so the apostrophe should be omitted.[20]

Students also often fail to recognize when a noun is being used in possessive form, and therefore incorrectly omit the apostrophe. Here is an example taken from the beginning of this chapter:

> Summary judgment should be granted in Defendants favor because the book meets the three-factor test under the work-for-hire doctrine.

The problem is that Defendant's requires an apostrophe plus *s* because the possessive form is being used.

2. Use with Words That End in S

Now the fun part: words that end with *s*.

Let's first distinguish two situations: The first is where a noun ends in an *s* because it is plural. With plural nouns, you add only an apostrophe after the *s* at the end of the plural noun.[21] Let's use defendants and plaintiffs. Let's say you have multiple defendants in a case, and you want to say, "Defendants' motion should be denied," you just put the apostrophe at the end. The same would be true if you wanted the Plaintiffs' motion to be denied.

The second situation is where a noun has a sibilant ending. A word with a sibilant ending just means that it ends with a hissing sound like a snake.[22] It can be a word that ends in *s* or *z* or *sh*. While journalists

---

20. As one legal writer aptly emphasized, "Despite what you see in a grocery store ad or on Twitter, almost never do you use an apostrophe to form a plural." Tenielle Fordyce-Ruff, *Back to the Basics: Apostrophes, Possession, and Contractions*, ADVOCATE, Aug. 2020, at 34, 35.

21. REDBOOK, *supra* note 8, at 142; Fordyce-Ruff, *supra* note 20, at 35.

22. *See Sibilant*, VOCABULARY.COM, https://www.vocabulary.com/dictionary/sibilant (last visited Apr. 2, 2022).

follow different rules for these words,[23] the *Redbook* makes it easy and creates a simple rule: Even if a *singular noun* ends in *s* or *ss*, you still use the apostrophe *s* ('s).[24] For example, one word you will often use in legal writing is "witness." If you are referring to a witness's testimony, you use the apostrophe *s* even though the word ends in *ss*.

Another example is the word "class" taken from my students' writing as referenced above:

> Student: Lannister created the Work because he thought it would improve his class' learning.
>
> Correct: Lannister created the Work because he thought it would improve his class's learning.

Lannister only taught one class, and class in this usage is a singular noun. So, one would add an apostrophe *s* at the end of the word. It does not matter that the word "class" ends in *ss*.

A final example of a common mistake I saw in my *Game of Thrones* problem was proper use of an apostrophe with "Westeros University." (Yes, I know there is no such thing). The "s" at the end caused confusion when students were using the possessive form, such as in this example:

> Student: In the shadow of Westeros' publishing culture, Lannister wrote the Work, which was applicable to the veteran student population in his classroom.

---

23. *The Chicago Manual of Style* provides that plural forms ending in *s* take an apostrophe only without a second *s*, such as United States' reputation. But singular forms, such as Kansas, take the apostrophe *s*. *Possessive of Proper Nouns, Abbreviations, and Numbers*, Chi. Manual of Style Online ch. 7.17, https://www.chicagomanualofstyle.org/book/ed17/part2/ch07/psec017.html (last visited Apr. 2, 2022). The manual also has exceptions. *The New York Times Manual of Style and Usage* provides similar guidelines but recommends omitting the *s* "when a word ends in two sibilant sounds… separated only by a vowel sound: *Kansas' Governor; Texas' population*." Allan M. Siegal & William G. Connolly, The New York Times Manual of Style and Usage 24 (Random House 1999). However, *Strunk & White*, like the *Redbook*, provides that you should add 's "whatever the final consonant" but has exceptions only for ancient proper names ending in -es and -s, such as "Jesus." William Strunk, Jr. & E. B. White, The Elements of Style 1 (4th ed., Longman 1999).

24. Redbook, *supra* note 8, at 142.

Since Westeros is a singular noun, even though it ends in *s*, the possessive form should be Westeros's, not Westeros'.

This rule about words ending in *s* doesn't change for proper nouns ending in *s*, such as James. If you are referring to his car, you say James's car.

But note that if you are trying to make a plural noun possessive, and that plural noun ends in "s" (as many do) then you do not add 's—instead, you just add the apostrophe after the *s*. For example, if you are talking about more than one witness, you would use the word "witnesses." To refer to testimony of the multiple witnesses, you would create the possessive by adding just the apostrophe at the end, without another *s*:

> The witnesses' testimony established....

Even though this rule seems simple enough, the courts do not always follow it.[25] More on that later.

3. Joint and Individual Possession

There is one little nuance on the possessive use of the apostrophe that we should address—that is, when you have two subjects doing something together or separately. If people did something together, you only make the final name in the series possessive. For example, if Julie and Jeff wrote a brief together you would refer to that with an apostrophe *s* at the end of both names, like this: "In Julie and Jeff's brief."[26]

On the other hand, if Julie and Jeff each wrote a separate brief for class, each name would be made possessive, like this: "In Julie's and Jeff's briefs."

4. Attorneys' Fees

Finally, let's discuss the controversy over *attorney's* fees vs. *attorneys'* fees. This comes up a lot in practice because in litigation a prevailing

---

25. Although I have covered the basic rules, there are some others worth mentioning. For example, if a singular name has a plural form, you use the apostrophe alone, such as in "the Court of Appeals' decision." REDBOOK, *supra* note 8, at 142. Also, although the *Redbook* states that some ancient names ending in a sibilant sound take the apostrophe alone, such as Moses', this is no longer the modern practice. *Id.*

26. FOGARTY, *supra* note 1, at 128; Betsy Six, *Illegal Possession*, J. KAN. BAR. ASSOC., Nov.–Dec. 2018, at 46, 47.

party is often trying to recover fees, and in contract drafting, lawyers will often include clauses regarding fees. I wish I had a clear answer for you on how to refer to this term, but no one can agree. The *Supreme Court Style Guide*, which sets the Court's style so that the Reporter of Decisions can prepare the Court's opinions for release to the public, says to use the singular "attorney's fees" rather than the plural "attorneys' fees," even when "more than one attorney may be involved."[27] Bryan Garner, however, believes that either attorney's fees or attorneys' fees is acceptable, and "attorneys' fees" is preferred where there is more than one attorney involved.[28] In contrast, Judge Lebovits recognizes that all variants of this phrase have their supporters, but recommends saying "attorney fees" because "by the law the fees belong to the client, not the attorney, and because 'attorney' in this context assumes both singular and plural."[29] The *California Style Manual* takes the same approach as Judge Lebovits, providing that the term "attorney fees" is preferred but stresses that whichever term is used "consistency within the document is required."[30] Ultimately, that is the best advice: if a style guide controls your situation, follow it. If it doesn't, check with your audience. If that doesn't work, be consistent in your approach, whatever it is.[31]

Now that you know the rules, you might be wondering if one little apostrophe could spark a dispute under the law. The answer is yes, it can, and it has. Some examples are discussed below.

---

27. The Supreme Court's Style Guide X–9 (Jack Metzler ed., interAlias Press 2016), https://budgetcounsel.files.wordpress.com/2018/10/supreme-courts-style-guide.pdf.

28. Bryan A. Garner, *LawProse Lesson #115: Is It Attorney's Fees or Attorneys' Fees?*, LawProse (Apr. 23, 2013) https://lawprose.org/lawprose-lesson-115-is-it-attorneys-fees-or-attorneys-fees/.

29. Lebovits, *supra* note 10, at 60.

30. Edward W. Jessen, California Style Manual § 4:60, at 163. (4th ed. 2000).

31. Kathy Sieckman, *Attorney's Fees or Attorneys' Fees?*, Proof That Blog (May 3, 2017), https://proofthatblog.com/2017/05/03/attorneys-fees-or-attorneys-fees/.

D. Apostrophes Become Embroiled in Lawsuits

In Florida—due solely to incorrect use of apostrophes creating an ambiguity—a court held that the party would not be allowed to recover attorney's fees.[32] (Notice where this court placed the apostrophe in attorney's fees.) Specifically, the attorney for one of the parties made what is called an offer of judgment to settle the case before trial. The attorney apparently used a form for doing so without editing it. It required, "Plaintiff'(s)" to "execute a stipulation," and "Plaintiff(s) to "execute" a general release of "Defendant(s)." The court stated that the offer was "apostrophe-challenged" and did not satisfy the particularity requirement.[33] Because it was unclear whether the drafter intended references to singular or plural defendants or plaintiffs, the court reversed a final judgment awarding attorney's fees.

An apostrophe also stirred up trouble when it appeared in a consent order, which is a cross between a contract (because it represents a compromise between parties in a case) and a court order (because it is enforced like a court order).[34] A consent order referring to the New York City Housing Authority (or NYCHA), in one place said "NYCHA public housing developments" and in another place said "NYCHA's public housing developments." The plaintiffs argued that the apostrophe *s* after NYCHA in the second sentence changed the meaning of that sentence, and a dispute arose about the meaning of the language in the consent order.[35] Although the court concluded that the apostrophe did not alter its meaning, the dispute might not have arisen without that apostrophe *s*.

E. The Political Side of Apostrophes

In addition to sparking litigation, the apostrophe has also sparked political controversy. In fact, the Sixth Circuit was apparently so enthralled by the politics of the apostrophe when it came to geographic names such

---

32. Bradshaw v. Boynton–JCP Assocs., 125 So. 3d 289, 290–91 (Fla. Dist. Ct. App. 2013).

33. *Id.*

34. Baez. v. N.Y.C. Hous. Auth., 533 F. Supp. 3d 135, 141 (S.D.N.Y. 2021).

35. *Id.* at 144–46.

as towns and cities, it discussed why the party in the case did not use an apostrophe, even though the case had nothing whatsoever to do with apostrophes (it had to do with the applicability of the Clean Air Act to a factory).[36]

One of the parties in the case was a factory called St. Marys Portland Cement, with no apostrophe in St. Marys. The court apparently believed it had to explain the absence of the apostrophe, so it noted that the company is based in Canada not far from the St. Marys River (also no apostrophe). The missing apostrophes in the company, the town, and a river were because the Geographic Board of Canada in 1898 discouraged the possessive form of place names to avoid suggesting private ownership of a public place.

Canada's struggles with the apostrophe don't end there. For example, in Quebec, Canada, the apostrophe is viewed as a sign of Anglo imperialism against French Canadians, and so pressure exists there to omit apostrophes.[37]

But you do not have to go as far as Canada to find an example of an apostrophe injecting itself into politics. You only have to go to Arkansas. In 2007, a state representative in Arkansas proposed a bill declaring that the possessive form of the state's name should be Arkansas's instead of Arkansas'.[38] It passed, and a non-binding resolution declared that the proper way to punctuate the possessive form of the state's name ends with an apostrophe *s*.[39] This sparked a "statewide civil war."[40]

People were upset for two reasons. First, the public was mad that the legislature had nothing better to do than pass bills about punctuation,

---

36. St. Marys Cement Inc. v. U.S. E.P.A., 782 F.3d 280, 282–84 (6th Cir. 2015).

37. Maureen Arrigo-Ward, Caring for Your Apostrophes, 4 Persp: Teaching Legal Rsch. & Writing 14, 15 (1995).

38. Paul Greenberg, *An Apostrophe Starts a War*, ARK. DEMOCRAT GAZETTE (March 4, 2007, 3:15 AM), https://www.arkansasonline.com/news/2007/mar/04/column-one-apostrophe-starts-war-20070304/. Apparently, this was not the first time that someone tried to do something about this issue. A federal appellate judge earlier had written a letter to the newspaper which had this heading under its name: Arkansas' Newspaper. The judge urged the paper to tack on an *s*. *Id.*

39. Nathan Bierma, *Possessive is Nine-Tenths Law in Arkansas's Statutes*, CHI. TRIB. (Apr. 5, 2007, 12:00 AM), https://www.chicagotribune.com/news/ct-xpm-2007-04-06-070 4040586-story.html.

40. Greenberg, *supra* note 38.

prompting an apology from its sponsor (the public had a point).[41] Second, the public disagreed that an apostrophe *s* should be added. The state's largest newspaper, the *Arkansas Democrat-Gazette* used the apostrophe-only form, and so did a journalism professor at the University of Arkansas.[42] Further, rules for journalists, including at the *Associated Press* and the *Chicago Tribune*, had mostly opted for the apostrophe-only approach.[43] *The Chicago Manual of Style* also allows (but does not prefer) the apostrophe-only approach. Thus, the apostrophe really stirred things up in Arkansas.

At this point, you are wondering what the highest courts in the land have to say about the Arkansas apostrophe issue. I'm glad you brought that up. In 1974, long before the so-called "Apostrophe Act of 2007,"[44] the U.S. Supreme Court used the apostrophe-only approach.[45] Referring to the state's constitution, it said: "Arkansas' Constitution."[46] Similarly, referring to exceptions to a master's report, it wrote: "Arkansas' exceptions to the report...."[47]

But fast forward to 2006, even before the apostrophe resolution was passed, where the Supreme Court of Arkansas used the apostrophe *s*, writing that the applicable statute of limitations is three years under "Arkansas's law."[48] Similarly, in 2021, the Supreme Court of Arkansas used the apostrophe-*s* approach, when referring to "Arkansas's sovereign immunity doctrine."[49] Therefore, at least with the courts in Arkansas, the apostrophe-*s* approach has caught on.

---

41. *See House Gets Possessive on the Letter 'S'*, Chi. Trib. (Mar. 6, 2007, 12:00 AM), https://www.chicagotribune.com/news/ct-xpm-2007-03-07-0703070052-story.html.

42. Bierma, *supra* note 39.

43. *Id.*

44. *Id.*

45. *See* Mississippi v. Arkansas, 415 U.S. 289, 290 (1974).

46. *Id.*

47. *Id.* at 291.

48. Ganey v. Kawasaki Motors Corp., USA, 234 S.W.3d 838, 841 (Ark. 2006), *overruled by* Lawson v. Simmons Sporting Goods, 569 S.W.3d 865 (2019).

49. Mahadevan v. Bd. of Trs., 633 S.W.3d 756, 758 (Ark. 2021).

F. The U.S. Supreme Court, the Apostrophe,
and Words Ending in S

Arkansas is not the only state presenting an apostrophe issue that has divided people. In fact, the Justices of the U.S. Supreme Court cannot even agree among themselves on how to form the possessive use of nouns that end in *s*. In *Kansas v. Marsh*,[50] the Justices not only splintered in deciding whether the death penalty statute in Kansas was constitutional, but also parted ways on whether the possessive use of Kansas should be "Kansas'" or "Kansas's." Writing for the majority, Justice Thomas (more on him later, as it pertains to the apostrophe), used just an apostrophe, referring to "Kansas' capital sentencing statute," "Kansas' procedure," and "Kansas' weighing equation."[51] Concurring, Justice Scalia "dissented" on the Kansas issue, preferring instead to use the apostrophe *s* referring to "Kansas's death penalty."[52] Justice Souter, joined by Justices Ginsburg and Breyer, dissented in the case but agreed with Justice Scalia, at least on the apostrophe issue, referring to "Kansas's capital sentencing statute."[53]

Therefore, even though the *Redbook* has a rule on this, and one that is easy to follow, that does not mean everyone is on board. In fact, one missing apostrophe *s* in Justice Thomas' name led some political scientists to research and write an article about the Supreme Court's use of the apostrophe.[54] Specifically, they studied Supreme Court opinions over 70 years to see whether it used the apostrophe *s* when referring to either proper or common nouns ending in *s*.[55] First, the researchers

---

50. 548 U.S. 163 (2006).

51. *Id.* 167, 175, 177.

52. *Id.* at 182 (Scalia, J., concurring). Interestingly, even though Justice Scalia added the apostrophe *s* for Kansas, he dropped the *s* when referring to Justice Stevens, writing, "Justice Stevens' contention." *Id.*

53. *Id.* at 203 (Souter, J., dissenting).

54. Ryan C. Black & Timothy R. Johnson, *Obsessive over the Possessive at the Supreme Court of the United States: Exploring SCOTUS'/SCOTUS's Use of Possessive Apostrophes*, 22 J. App. Prac. & Process 13, 13–14 (2022).

55. *Id.* at 14–15. An earlier study of this topic focused on the 2014–2015 term concluded that "The Justices have long disagreed on whether a singular word ending in *s* should get a lone apostrophe or an apostrophe-plus-*s* to indicate the possessive." Jill Barton, *Supreme Court Splits… on Grammar and Writing Style*, 17 Scribes J. Legal Writing 33, 41 (2017).

analyzed opinions where Justices with last names ending in *s* referred to each other.[56] Justice Holmes was the most-cited Justice with 195 references, and 171 of those used the *s* apostrophe (the single *s*) compared to only 24 uses of the apostrophe *s* (the double *s*). The political scientists next studied the word "Congress" to see whether the Court referred to Congress' or Congress's.[57] Analyzing more than 70 terms' worth of Supreme Court opinions, the authors concluded that 30 of the 39 Justices demonstrated a strong preference for the single *s* possessive (Congress' not Congress's).[58] They also explained, however, that their data supported a new trend because more recent opinions indicated the Court is moving toward a double *s* possessive when referring to Congress.

Therefore, although the *Redbook* has created a clear and simple rule to follow for sibilant endings, the Supreme Court is torn on the topic but appears to be trending toward using apostrophe *s*—the double *s*—with sibilant endings.

As you have seen, one small punctuation mark can create lots of trouble. Know how to use the apostrophe as a contraction and to form the possessive use, and do not confuse the two uses. By now, if you go back to the incorrect sentences at the beginning of this chapter, you should be able to spot the problems and correct them. Finally, remember that no matter what method you choose, consistency is key.

---

56. Black & Johnson, *supra* note 54, at 22–23.
57. *Id.* at 24.
58. *Id.* at 26.

"Wait— I thought I asked for a small-animal veterinarian."

Purple People-Eaters, Muttons, and Nuts

Hyphens, Em Dashes, and En Dashes¹

Y ou know what a hyphen is and where to find it on your keyboard. But be honest. Do you know what a purple people-eater has to do with hyphens? What about em dashes? Can you explain when to use an em dash and where to find it on your keyboard? What about the en dash? Don't worry. You are not alone. (Admission #1: I had never even heard of em dashes or en dashes until I started teaching legal writing.)

We are going to discuss hyphens, em dashes, and en dashes not just because most students are not sure what these different marks are or how to use them, but because, just like the other punctuation and grammar rules in this book, proper use will help distinguish you as an excellent legal writer—and misuse can hurt your credibility as an advocate.

Life was much simpler before my revelation about these three marks (I would call them dashes, but a hyphen is not strictly a dash). I thought all dashes were hyphens and that was that (and that was wrong). But now that I know about them, I am constantly racked with anxiety: Is this

---

1. The *Redbook* places a hyphen after the words em- and en- and before the word "dash." *See* Bryan A. Garner, The Redbook: A Manual on Legal Style 43–45 (4th ed. 2018) [hereinafter Redbook]. But *Dreyer's English* does not include the hyphen. Benjamin Dreyer, Dreyer's English 62 (2019). The *ALWD Guide* also does not use the hyphen. Carolyn V. Williams, Ass'n of Legal Writing Dirs., ALWD Guide to Legal Citation 23 (Wolters Kluwer 7th ed.) [hereinafter ALWD]. Neither does the *Bluebook*. The Bluebook: A Uniform System of Citation R. 3.2(a), at 74 (Columbia L. Rev. Ass'n et al. eds, 21st ed. 2020) [hereinafter Bluebook]. Because the dictionary does not use them either, I have chosen to use these terms without hyphens. *E.g. Em Dash*, Lexico, https://www.lexico.com/en/definition/em_dash (last visited Feb. 9, 2022). This is another example where people just cannot get along when it comes to when to use a hyphen and when not to.

a case for a hyphen or an en dash? I would love to put a dash here, but aren't I supposed to avoid em dashes? (Admission #2: my usage of em dashes has greatly increased, and I fear I am getting addicted.)

Before we go any further, here are the three marks:

    Hyphen: -
    En dash: –
    Em dash: —

The physical distinction is easy—length. The hyphen is the Muggsy Bogues (the shortest basketball player in NBA history) of punctuation: it is the shortest of the marks. The em dash is the Yao Ming of punctuation (okay, he is not the tallest basketball player ever to play the game, but he is close to it). The en dash is in the middle between Muggsy Bogues and Yao Ming. But the rules for use are not so easy.

A. Hyphens and Purple People-Eaters

I like to think of the hyphen as the dash that is used *within, or to combine,* words. While that may sound simple, you may be surprised to learn that the hyphen is probably the most volatile of the three marks because when to use it is both controversial[2] and constantly in flux.[3] Its use is declining; it has been in therapy to deal with its loss of popularity. Sadly (for the hyphen), people have wanted to abolish the hyphen for years,[4] and dictionaries are starting to listen.[5] In 2007, thousands of hyphens perished when a new edition of the *Shorter Oxford English Dictionary* eliminated hyphens in 16,000 words. For example, "fig-leaf" became "fig leaf," and bumble-bee became "bumblebee." If you are wondering how a punctuation mark can become extinct, blame yourself and the proliferation of communication through emails and texts. Simply speaking, the hyphen is seen as "old-fashioned" and people "are not con-

---

2. *See* Joan Ames Magat, *Hawking Hyphens in Compound Modifiers*, 11 Legal Comm. & Rhetoric: JALWD 153 (2014).

3. *See* Finto Rohrer, *Small Object of Grammatical Desire*, BBC News (Sept. 20, 2007), news.bbc.co.uk/2/hi/uk_news/magazine/7004661.stm.

4. Lynne Truss, Eats, Shoots, & Leaves 168 (Gotham Books 2004).

5. Simon Rabinovitch, *Thousands of Hyphens Perish as English Marches On*, Reuters (Sept. 21, 2007), https://www.reuters.com/article/us-britain-hyphen-1/thousands-of-hyphens-perish-as-english-marches-on-idUSHAR15384620070921.

fident about using hyphens anymore."[6] Dictionaries only reflect what people are reading and writing, and when hyphen usage drops, dictionaries follow suit.[7] Did you know you had that kind of power?

Does that mean you can skip learning when to use a hyphen? That was a rhetorical question.

Do courts care about hyphens? Yes, they do.[8] In fact, in an interview in 2010 with Supreme Court Justice Antonin Scalia, he was asked why he was so finicky in hyphenating phrasal adjectives in his opinions, and his response included a reference to purple people-eaters:

> I was on the *Harvard Law Review* in the days when we had a *Bluebook* that was taken very seriously. And we had things called the "unit-modifier rule." It is a rule that really does make a lot of sense, and the example that we always used to use was the "purple people eater." If it's a purple eater of people, you would write it "purple people, hyphen, eater," right? And you would understand that: a purple people-eater. On the other hand, if it was an eater of purple people, the hyphen would be moved over: "purple-people eater." It helps comprehension, and anything that helps comprehension should be embraced.[9]

Therefore, if you write about purple people eaters, you need to be clear about who is eating who. Let's use another example where the use of a hyphen (or not) can create ambiguity.

Let's say you want to talk about a shark and a man. You could say, "I saw a man-eating shark," or you could say, "I saw a man eating shark." Do you see the difference one hyphen can make? The first sentence is referring to a type of shark, while the second phrase is talking about a man eating something. The hyphen resolves the ambiguity. You might

---

6. *Id.*

7. Rohrer, *supra* note 3.

8. For example, the Supreme Court of Washington devoted an entire opinion to a discussion of a hyphen appearing on a check payable to "Rick Knight-Simplot Soil Builders." *See* J.R. Simplot, Inc. v. Knight, 988 P.2d 955 (Wash. 1999). Although the court concluded that the hyphen was ambiguous, it ultimately held that the intent was to allow the check to be endorsed by either payee. *Id.* at 960.

9. *Interviews with United States Supreme Court Justices: Justice Antonin Scalia*, 13 SCRIBES JOURNAL of LEGAL WRITING 51, 63 (2010).

not often refer to man-eating sharks in legal writing, but you will refer to sharks when talking about lawyers in general (or, to be precise, when telling a lawyer joke).

B. When to Use a Hyphen and When Not To

Before getting into some helpful dos and don'ts, to quote author Lynne Truss, "hyphen usage is just a big bloody mess and is likely to get messier."[10] In fact, many style guides outside of legal writing seem to take the view that instead of creating a black and white rule for when to use hyphens in compound words, they should be used only when the meaning would be unclear.[11] The man-eating shark/man eating shark example would be one of those situations.

But courts do not always agree on whether to use a hyphen, even in important matters, such as references to legal doctrines. One such doctrine is the "work for hire" doctrine under copyright law. Essentially, that doctrine provides that if an employee creates a work (which can be a computer program, a book, a film, etc.) within the course and scope of that employee's employment, the copyright belongs to the employer.[12] Discussing the work for hire doctrine, courts have taken varying approaches on whether to place hyphens when referring to the doctrine: is it work-for-hire or work for hire? For example, the United States Supreme Court used no hyphens when referring to the work for hire doctrine in *Community for Creative Non-Violence v. Reid*.[13] In contrast, in a different case, the Ninth Circuit used hyphens when it wrote that the district court had found that the plaintiff owned the software program under the "work-for-hire doctrine."[14]

Among legal writing scholars, there is no general consensus on when to use hyphens, prompting the *Redbook* to stress that "the hyphen gives writers more trouble than any other punctuation mark," and "generates

---

10. TRUSS, *supra* note 4, at 176.

11. *E.g.*, Magat, *supra* note 2, at 154–55; ALLAN M. SIEGAL & WILLIAM G. CONNOLLY, THE NEW YORK TIMES MANUAL OF STYLE AND USAGE 163 (Random House 1999).

12. Cmty. for Creative Non-Violence v. Reid, 490 U.S. 730, 737 (1989); 17 U.S.C. § 201(b).

13. 490 U.S. 730, 737 ("The contours of the work for hire doctrine therefore carry profound significance....").

14. JustMed, Inc. v. Byce, 600 F.3d 1118, 1120 (9th Cir. 2010).

some controversy."[15] That could be why improper hyphen usage is one of the most common mistakes in legal writing.[16] Judge Lebovits, a prolific author on legal writing issues, gives the example of the "criminal justice system." If you leave out the hyphen between criminal and justice, it sounds like you are saying our justice system is "criminal," so he advises to use a hyphen when referring to the criminal-justice system.

Given that the use of hyphens is so subjective, can you just use your own system and stop reading here? That is another rhetorical question.

Here are some general guidelines:

- Include hyphens within a phrasal adjective (unless an exception applies).

A phrasal adjective, also referred to as a compound adjective or a compound modifier, is a phrase that functions as an adjective. When several words *together* modify or describe a noun, and they only make sense together as an adjective modifying a noun, the phrase is ordinarily hyphenated.

Let's take an example: **small animal veterinarian vs. small-animal veterinarian.** Which makes sense? Are you talking about a veterinarian that is the size of Muggsy Bogues or are you talking about a veterinarian that specializes in caring for small animals? Because the absence of the hyphen results in an ambiguity, you need the hyphen. Look again at Justice Scalia's quotation above and you will see this is the same rule he uses to explain the purple people eater example.

The tricky thing here is that there are exceptions to this rule, so bear with me. You should not hyphenate a phrasal adjective that begins with an -ly adverb (which modifies a verb, adverb, or adjective) unless the phrase is longer than two words.[17]

Here are examples:

Two Word Phrasal Adjective: **The student made a highly effective argument in the moot court competition.** No hyphen is needed between highly and effective (two words).

---

15. REDBOOK, *supra* note 1, at 47.

16. Gerald Lebovits, *The Worst Mistakes in Legal Writing—Part II*, N.Y. St. BAR Ass'n J., Mar. 2018, at 62, 64.

17. REDBOOK, *supra* note 1, at 48.

Phrasal Adjective of More than Two Words: **The student made a poorly-thought-out argument.** You need the hyphen here because the phrase "poorly-thought-out" is longer than two words.

Also, remember that you do not need a hyphen if the phrasal adjective comes *after* the noun it modifies. Let's go back to the work-for-hire doctrine (or work for hire doctrine if you follow the Supreme Court's lead). Take this example: "Congress passed a statute that incorporated a doctrine known as work for hire." No hyphen is needed because the phrasal adjective (work for hire) comes *after* the noun (doctrine). Here's another example: "The well-settled doctrine favors plaintiff's position here," compared to "the doctrine plaintiff has relied upon is well settled." Well settled is hyphenated when it precedes the noun "doctrine" but is not hyphenated when it comes after the noun.

Some other uses of the hyphen:

- Include a hyphen with numbers to join two-word *spelled out* numbers from 21–99 and to write fractions unless one of the numbers is already hyphenated.[18]

  Here is an example: He ate **three-fourths** of the pie at Thanksgiving.

- Use hyphens to break a word between syllables at the end of a line.

- Use hyphens when using certain prefixes, although modern usage omits most hyphens after prefixes.[19]

  If you write "precursor," you do not need a hyphen, but when the root word is a proper noun, such as anti-Semitic, you do need a hyphen. Also, in general, use a hyphen with most words beginning with "all," "ex", and "self." For example, take this statement: "He made a self-serving statement about how the light was green when he went through the intersection."

---

18. *Id.* at 51.
19. *Id.* at 52.

- Do not use hyphens if a proper noun is being used as an adjective.[20]

  Here is an example: The *Stone v. State* case was a landmark case. The phrase, "*Stone v. State*" is a phrasal adjective of more than two words, but because it is a proper noun, you do not use hyphens to connect the words.

If you are having trouble keep track of these rules, then follow this general piece of advice: consult a dictionary or other reference book to see if the word should be hyphenated.[21] And remember that most professional writers, legal writers, and judges prefer hyphens especially where one is needed to make sure the meaning is clear. If that doesn't work, just ask whether you are writing about purple people-eaters or man-eating sharks.

C. Em Dashes

In sharp contrast to the hyphen, which is losing customers, the em dash is gaining customers and is wildly popular in some circles. They are called "em" because they were originally the width of a typesetter's capital "M" (though they are a smidge wider now).[22] An old nickname for them was the "mutton dash."[23] (That did not seem to catch on, so I would avoid using it if you want people to know what you are referring to unless, of course, it's the answer to a question in some trivia game.) The em dash (the Yao Ming of the dashes) basically substitutes for a full range of punctuation marks, such as a comma, a colon, a semicolon, and parentheses. It is especially popular in today's world of quick bursts of communication in things like texts and tweets.[24]

---

20. *Id.* at 48.

21. The *Redbook* also has a lengthy list of words and phrases commonly used in legal writing that require hyphens. *Id.* at 49–51.

22. DREYER, *supra* note 1, at 62; *Dash*, STRAIGHT FORWARD: QUIRKY LETTERS (Sept. 7, 2018) https://straightforward.design/posters/dash/.

23. *Dash: Em Dash*, WIKIPEDIA, https://en.wikipedia.org/wiki/Dash#Em_dash (last visited Feb. 10, 2022); STRAIGHT FORWARD, *supra* note 22.

24. Kate Mooney, *The Em Dash Divides*, N.Y. TIMES (Aug. 14, 2019), https://www.nytimes.com/2019/08/14/style/em-dash-punctuation.html.

1. Opposing Views of Em Dashes

Despite its versatility, the em dash has its detractors. Some see it as the "enemy of grammar"[25] because it shows up in informal communications, such as texts and tweets. It is generally thought of as a mark that is used in more casual situations; you would not bring it with you to black tie affair.[26] Strunk & White advise to use it "only when a more common mark of punctuation seems inadequate."[27] In *Grammar Girl*, Mignon Fogarty, describing the em dash as "dramatic," recommends using them only when a statement is important or dramatic.[28] It also disrupts the flow of a sentence, so some writers do not like that aspect of it.[29] Given that we are already so distracted as we go back and forth between screens, conversations, and texts, do we really need a mark that serves to further distract us? Apparently so.

The em dash has staunch support among writers in general. Poet Emily Dickinson was known as a frequent customer of the em dash in her writing.[30] Author R.L. Stine (known as the Stephen King of children's literature and author of the *Goosebumps* series) also uses them frequently because when a moment of true horror arrives in a novel, the em dash is the way to go.[31] Author Tom Wolfe also loves them because they imitate the habits of actual thought in that we do not think in complete sentences.[32] Simply speaking, authors like them because "they know *you*

25. TRUSS, *supra* note 4, at 157.

26. WILLIAM STRUNK JR. & E.B. WHITE, THE ELEMENTS OF STYLE 9 (4th ed. Longman, 1999) (describing it as "mark of separation stronger than a comma, less formal than a colon, and more relaxed than parentheses.").

27. *Id.*

28. MIGNON FOGARTY, GRAMMAR GIRL'S QUICK & DIRTY TIPS FOR BETTER WRITING 95–96 (2008).

29. Noreen Malone, *The Case—Please Hear Me out—Against the Em Dash*, SLATE (May 24, 2011, 4:32 PM), https://slate.com/human-interest/2011/05/em-dashes-why-writers-should-use-them-more-sparingly.html

30. *Id.*

31. Emily Temple, *The Punctuation Marks Loved (and Hated) by Famous Writers*, LITERARY HUB (MAY 4, 2021), https://lithub.com/the-punctuation-marks-loved-and-hated-by-famous-writers/.

32. *Id.*

can't use it wrongly—which for a punctuation mark, is an uncommon virtue."[33]

2. Legal Writers Use Em Dashes

Legal writers also like em dashes; even Supreme Court Justices use them. I think that means you have permission to use them.[34] Chief Justice Roberts used em dashes in *Riley v. California*,[35] as follows: "The defendants here recognize—indeed, they stress—that such fact-specific threats may justify a warrantless search of cell phone data."[36] Justices Scalia and Breyer have also used them, including in dissenting opinions, leading one author who surveyed Supreme Court opinions and the use of emphatic devices such as em dashes to conclude that "dissenting Justices use [em dashes and italics] far more than their winning counterparts."[37]

It is not only Supreme Court Justices that use em dashes; lawyers writing to the Supreme Court use them as well. In fact, if you are ever bored, one fun thing to do is count the number of sentences using em dashes in briefs filed with the Supreme Court. In a relatively short, 12-page brief filed in 2021 with the Supreme Court by attorneys general representing some 13 states, lawyers wrote 16 sentences that included em dashes.[38] Here are just a few examples of sentences from that brief using em dashes:

> "That cannot be—and is not—the law."[39]

> "That is because none existed and *no one*—not petitioners, respondents, the United States or any of the amici—thought that

---

33. *Cf.* Truss, *supra* note 4, at 122.

34. Still, do not overuse them. *See* Stacy Rogers Sharp, *Crafting Responses to Counterarguments*, 10 Legal Comm. & Rhetoric: JALWD 201, 223 (2013) ("[E]m dashes ... are recommended as only an occasional emphatic device.").

35. 573 U.S. 373, 402 (2014).

36. *Id.*

37. Sharp, *supra* note 34, at 223–24.

38. Reply Brief for State Petitioners at 1–2, 4–11, Arizona v. City & Cnty. of S.F., No. 20-1775 (Sept. 8, 2021) 2021 WL 4135137 at *1–2, *4–11.

39. *Id.* at 5, 2021 WL 4135137 at *5.

petitioners could only have validly intervened if they had unique defenses of their own to raise."[40]

"Unlike the taxpayer in *Donaldson*, the Petitioners here have legally protectable interests—monetary interests and procedural rights under the APA—that justify their intervention in this case."[41]

That is a lot of energy and drama in one brief! In other words, legal writers often use em dashes, and they appear to be on the rise.[42]

3. Guidelines for Usage

Now that you have learned that legal writers use them, here are some guidelines to help ensure you use them correctly.

Use to Change Emphasis
- Using an em dash instead of a colon
   Example with Colon: A writing professor is mainly interested in three things: accuracy, brevity, and clarity.
   Example with Em Dash: A writing professor is mainly interested in three things—accuracy, brevity, and clarity.

In general, the em dash is less formal than the colon, and it puts more emphasis on the information after the dash than a colon does.

- Using em dashes instead of commas
   Example with commas: When she finally got the job offer, which she did not receive until six months after her interview, she had already accepted a job with another firm.

---

40. *Id.* at 6–7, 2021 WL 4135137 at *6–7.

41. *Id.* at 7, 2021 WL 4135137 at *7.

42. John H. Ridge, *Common Writing Rules I Commonly Forget, Part Three*, Wyo. Law., June 2018, at 52, 52. Em dashes, and how their use impacts the meaning of a statute, have also been the subject of court opinions. *See, e.g.*, United States v. Howell, No. 20-cr-30075-1, 2021 WL 2000245, at *3 (C.D. Ill. May 19, 2021) (noting that "the presence of an em dash before a list in statutory language indicates that the word or phrase preceding the dash" should be interpreted "to modify each of the succeeding list items individually.").

Example with em dashes: When she finally got the job offer—which she did not receive until six months after her interview—she had already accepted a job with another firm.

Again, the use of em dashes puts more emphasis on the material within the em dashes than commas do.

- Using em dashes instead of parentheses

  Example with parentheses: The legal writing professor (after discovering 50 citation errors) told the student that corrections had to be made before the memo could be submitted as a writing sample.

  Example with em dashes: The legal writing professor—after discovering 50 citation errors—told the student that corrections had to be made before the memo could be submitted as a writing sample.

As with the uses of the em dash in the above examples, the use of em dashes instead of parentheses serves to add more emphasis. While parentheses tend to minimize the information contained within them, em dashes serve the opposite function.[43]

- Using an em dash instead of a semicolon

An em dash can also replace a semicolon to merge two independent clauses—clauses that can stand alone as sentences.

  Example with semicolon: By paying close attention to the writing professor's instructions, the student did an excellent job; he received an A in the class and produced a great writing sample.

  Example with em dash: By paying close attention to the writing professor's instructions, the student did an excellent job—he received an A in the class and produced a great writing sample.

Use to Change Direction of Thought

Another common use of em dashes is to indicate an interruption or change of thought,[44] such as in this example:

---

43. REDBOOK, *supra* note 1, at 43.

44. Gerald Lebovits, *Do's, Don'ts, and Maybes: Legal Writing Punctuation—Part III*, N.Y. ST. BAR ASS'N J., May 2018, at 64, 54.

I was late to class—I think it was a week ago—because my car would not start.

Use to Indicate Missing Information

The final reason for using an em dash in legal writing is to indicate certain omissions. It might also be used to omit part of someone's name to preserve anonymity or to avoid spelling out an obscenity.

Here is an example: This iPhone is six years old and is a piece of s—.

Miscellaneous Rules

- Never use an en dash or hyphen when you mean to use an em dash. People will notice. The em dash is the looooong one. In general, avoid using more than two in a sentence.[45]

4. How to Insert an Em Dash

Now that you know how to use them, let's briefly cover how to insert them. Inserting an em dash is a pain in the a— compared to a hyphen, which can be found right on the keyboard. In fact, I am quite sure I would use em dashes more if they were easier to insert into my writing.

There are three main ways to create an em dash in Microsoft Word.[46]

Double Hyphen: After typing a word, but before tapping the space bar, insert two hyphens, and then immediately (again without tapping the space bar) type the next word. Your word-processing program will automatically turn those two hyphens into an em dash, with proper spacing before and after the words.

Insert Symbol. The next way is to go to Insert, then Symbol, and select Special Characters and you will see "em dash" in the list—of course, the em dash thinks it is special. Select the em dash and press insert.[47]

---

45. *Em Dash,* Punctuation Guide, https://www.thepunctuationguide.com/em-dash.html (last visited Feb. 10, 2022).

46. These guidelines are based upon Microsoft Word for Office 365.

47. In this menu that you can create your own em dash shortcut by pressing "Shortcut Key, entering whatever key combination you like in the "Press new shortcut key" box, and

Alt 0151. On your keyboard you can also press the "Alt" key and hold it while typing "0151" on the number pad. When you release the ALT key, an em dash will appear. If this one doesn't work for you at first, check to make sure "Num Lock" is on.

If you're a Mac user—I'm not, but I won't hold it against you—I'm told that you can create an em dash by pressing "Option + Shift + Hyphen" on your keyboard.[48]

Em dashes are like a pair of tennis shoes. They go with just about anything; they are a casual alternative to the more traditional punctuation marks. Their most common and effective use is to provide emphasis in your writing, but be careful not to overuse them. Be strategic.

D. En Dashes

En dashes are introverted compared to em dashes. They are the wallflowers, while the em dashes are the partiers. They are called en dashes because they were originally the width of an N.[49] Long ago, they were nicknamed "nuts,"[50] although like the nickname "muttons" for em dashes, that nickname is not used by many (so maybe keep that piece of information to yourself).

Essentially, the en dash substitutes for the word "to."[51] Sometimes, en dashes sit between numbers where the meaning is "up to and including" in a span or range, like this:

The plaintiff was a longtime employee and worked there for ten years (2010–2020).

You might also use an en dash to express a span of large numbers, or with a range of monetary amounts, like this:

---

then hitting "Assign." You can use this function to create a shortcut for *any* symbol that your keyboard doesn't want you to know about. But this is an advanced word-processing maneuver that you perform at your own risk.

48. *See, e.g.,* Justin Pot, *Your Keyboard Doesn't Have an Em Dash Key—Here's What To Do,* ZAPIER: APP TIPS (Oct. 12, 2020), https://zapier.com/blog/em-dash-on-keyboard/.

49. *Dash: En Dash,* WIKIPEDIA, https://en.wikipedia.org/wiki/Dash#En_dash (last visited Feb. 11, 2022).

50. STRAIGHT FORWARD, *supra* note 22.

51. Elizabeth Ruiz Frost, *Decoding Hyphens, Dashes and Ellipses,* OR. ST. BAR BULL., July 2015, at 13, 14.

Associates at this firm make about $160,000–$180,000.

You should not use an en dash mixed with the words "from… to" or "between… and."[52] In that situation, "the construction doesn't 'read' correctly if the understood word *to* or *and* is mentally voiced."[53]

Here is an example:

WRONG: She taught legal writing from 1994–2022.

RIGHT: She taught legal writing at the law school 1994–2022.

RIGHT: She taught legal writing from 1994 to 2022.

You might also use an en dash to express game scores[54] and court decisions,[55] such as writing, "Duke beat Kentucky, 96–95" or "The court voted 6–2 to uphold the lower court's ruling."

Because you use en dashes to express page ranges, you will often use them to express what are called "pinpoint citations" or "pin cites." If you do not know what these are, you will very soon. While style guides now give you the option of using either hyphens or en dashes when express- ing page ranges[56] check the style guide that controls your submissions, as it might call for a different requirement. For example, the Supreme Court requires that *only* en dashes should be used for page ranges.[57]

Let's give you an example of page ranges using an en dash and one using a hyphen.

With hyphen: *J.R. Simplot, Inc. v. Knight*, 988 P.2d 955, 958-59 (Wash. 1999).

With en dash: *J.R. Simplot, Inc. v. Knight*, 988 P.2d 955, 958–59 (Wash. 1999).

---

52. REDBOOK, *supra* note 1, at 45.

53. *Id.*

54. DREYER, *supra* note 1, at 64; REDBOOK, *supra* note 1, at 46.

55. REDBOOK, *supra* note 1, at 46.

56. ALWD, *supra* note 1, at 22 (directing writers to join the beginning and ending page numbers of a span with a hyphen, en dash, or the word "to"); BLUEBOOK, *supra* note 1, at 74 ("When citing material that spans more than one page, give the inclusive page numbers, separated by an en dash (–) or hyphen (-).").

57. *See* THE SUPREME COURT'S STYLE GUIDE I–4 (Jack Metzler ed., interAlias Press 2016).

You might think that in all of the above examples you could have used a hyphen. After all, can someone really tell the different between and dash that looks like this - and one that looks like this – ? While I have not found any research on the subject, my guess is that most people do in fact use a hyphen in those cases for three reasons: first, most people don't even know what an en dash is; second, it is virtually impossible to detect a difference in appearance; and third, it is much easier to insert a hyphen than an en dash. But now you know the difference and will not make that mistake, unless, of course, the governing rules allow you to use either one.

1. How to Insert an En Dash

Insert Symbol. Go to Insert, then Symbol, and select Special Characters and you will see en dash in the list—of course, the em dash appears before the en dash because it is a bit conceited. Ignore the em dash, select the en dash, and press insert.

Alt 0150. On your keyboard you can also press the "Alt" key and hold it while typing "0150." When you release the ALT key, an en dash will appear.

For Mac users, just take one hand off your half-caff cold-brew oat milk mochaccino and use it to press the "Option + Hyphen" keys.[58]

In conclusion, hyphens, em dashes, and en dashes have different uses and purposes. Hyphen usage is declining, but em dash usage is increasing. En dashes, poor things, do not have a significant role in legal writing, but they do play some part, so now you know when to use those as well.

---

58. Pot, *supra* note 48.

7

Three Nouns Walk into a Bar

I n case you have not guessed, in this chapter we will cover some key issues on matching pronouns with nouns. A pronoun is a word that stands in for a noun. The noun usually comes before the pronoun, and the pronoun must agree in number, gender, and person with that noun.[1] Although this rule seems rather simple, it can get complicated with some nouns. First, we will cover nouns and situations that call for an *it* pronoun. Second, we will cover the use of the word *they* to refer to a singular noun. Finally, we will cover how to write to a court in a way that respects gender identities.

A. Using "It"

I have seen law students who are confused when deciding what pronoun to use when it comes to words—called "collective nouns"—such as "court," "corporation," or "company." Often, students use the word *they* to refer to these nouns perhaps because they consist of more than one thing, but that is incorrect.[2] The correct pronoun to use with these nouns is *it*. (Unless, of course, you are referring to the plural noun, such as courts or companies, and then you would use *they*.) And use of *it* in this instance, although it has an impersonal aura, is not in any way disrespectful or insensitive.[3]

---

1. Bryan A. Garner, The Redbook: A Manual on Legal Style 200–01 (4th ed. 2018) [hereinafter Redbook].

2. Heidi K. Brown, *Get with the Pronoun*, 17 Legal Comm. & Rhetoric: JALWD 61, 61 (2020) ("Legal writing professors and law office supervisors have, for decades, corrected novice legal writers' use of the word *they* to refer to 'the court' or 'the company' or the 'the government.'").

3. *Id.*

The word *collective* means "of or characteristic of a group of individuals taken together."[4] A collective noun is a noun that is written in singular form but denotes a group of persons or objects. Hence, there is confusion: Do collective nouns call for a singular pronoun, such as *it*, or a plural pronoun, such as *they*? In most cases, collective nouns use a pronoun such as *it* and *its* instead of *they*, *them*, or *their*.[5] That's because *collective nouns* refer to a group of multiple people or things as a single unit or entity.

This issue comes up frequently in legal writing because lawyers routinely write about collective nouns, such as a jury, a court, a board, a majority, Congress, government, etc. All these nouns should be paired with *it* or *its*.

For example, here are a few statements from an opinion of the United States Supreme Court, which use *it* to describe a court and Congress:

> On remand, the District *Court* again struck down the 2016 Plan.... *It* found standing and concluded that the case was appropriate for judicial resolution.[6]

> The standards proposed by the President and the Solicitor General—if applied outside the context of privileged information—would risk seriously impeding *Congress* in carrying out *its* responsibilities.[7]

Confusion can arise, however, because sometimes collective nouns act as a unit, but sometimes collective nouns spread their wings and act separately as individuals.[8]

Example where the class is acting individually: The class arrived at various times because *they* forgot to set their clocks back.

---

4. *Collective*, Dictionary.com, https://www.dictionary.com/browse/collective (last visited Mar. 6, 2022).

5. Wayne Schiess, *Collective Nouns: Singular or Plural?*, Univ. Tex. Austin Blog Serv.: Legible (June 5, 2017), https://sites.utexas.edu/legalwriting/2017/06/05/collective-nouns-singular-or-plural/.

6. Rucho v. Common Cause, 139 S. Ct. 2484, 2492 (2019).

7. Trump v. Mazars, USA, LLP, 140 S. Ct. 2019, 2033 (2020).

8. *See* Redbook, *supra* note 1, at 203.

Example where the class is acting as a unit: The class was excellent; *it* really boosted my spirits every time I taught.

Example where the jury is acting individually: The jury members disagreed about the guilt of the accused and told the judge that *they* were hopelessly deadlocked.

Example where the jury is acting as a unit: After four days of deliberation, the jury finally delivered *its* verdict: the defendant was guilty.

Therefore, when you refer to a court, something you will do often, or any other collective noun acting as a unit, use *it*, not *they*.

B. "It" with Non-Humans

The pronoun *it* is also used when the noun is not human. For example, here are more Supreme Court statements where the Court uses *it* when referring to a noun:

Partisan gerrymandering is nothing new. Nor is frustration with *it*.[9]

The First Amendment test simply describes the act of districting for partisan advantage. *It* provides no standard for determining when partisan activity goes too far.[10]

Now that you understand *it*, let's move on to *they* as a singular pronoun.

C. Using "They" as a Singular Pronoun[11]

What do I mean by using *they* as a singular pronoun? Let's say you are writing about the hesitancy of law students, in general, to take classes that start early in the morning. You might write something like this:

A law *student* might not take legal writing if *they* find out the class starts at 8:00 a.m.

---

9. *Rucho,* 139 S. Ct. at 2494.

10. *Id.* at 2504.

11. To be clear, this section is not referring to the situation where a person is non-binary and is a "they." That will be addressed in the last part of this chapter.

In that example, the word "student" is a singular noun—a noun identifying one object or person—and *they* is being used as a "singular pronoun" because it substitutes for a singular noun, or *one* object or person. The question is whether the use of *they* with a singular noun is considered proper grammar.

Using *they* as a singular pronoun is not a new idea. In fact, that usage "is not an innovation of recent decades or even of this century."[12] In *Pride and Prejudice*, which Jane Austen wrote in 1813, the singular *they* (or its possessive, their) appears 75 times.[13] Here is just one example:

> You wanted me, I know, to say "Yes," that you might have the pleasure of despising my taste; but I always delight in overthrowing those kind of schemes, and cheating a person of *their* premeditated contempt.[14]

And while we might think that using the singular *they* just recently became a hot topic in legal writing circles, as early as 1996, at least one legal writer advocated for the singular *they*.[15]

Is use of *they* as a singular pronoun acceptable? Let's take a poll. President Biden is on board. Just after he was inaugurated, he signed an executive order on gender identity and sexual orientation discrimination, which used the singular *they*:

> Every person should be treated with respect and dignity and should be able to live without fear, no matter who *they* are or whom they love.[16]

Even beyond the White House, the U.S. Supreme Court has also used the singular *they*. In *Lockhart v. United States*,[17] Justice Sotomayor, joined

---

12. Robert D. Eagleson, *A Singular Use of They*, 5 Scribes J. Legal Writing 87, 89 (1996).

13. Lorraine Berry, *"They": the Singular Pronoun that Could Solve Sexism in English*, Guardian (May 5, 2016, 7:00 AM), https://www.theguardian.com/books/booksblog/2016/may/05/they-the-singular-pronoun-that-could-solve-sexism-in-english.

14. *List of Examples of Singular "Their," Etc. from Jane Austen's Writings*, Republic Pemberley, https://pemberley.com/janeinfo/austhlis.html (last visited Mar. 6, 2022).

15. *See generally* Eagleson, *supra* note 12.

16. Exec. Order No. 13,988, 86 Fed. Reg. 7023, 7023 (Jan. 20, 2021).

17. 577 U.S. 347 (2016).

by Chief Justice Roberts, and Justices Kennedy, Thomas, Ginsburg, and Alito (note that this list includes both liberal and conservative Justices), wrote this statement using the singular *they* in the majority opinion:

> Section 2262(b)(2)'s list is hardly the way an average person, or even an average lawyer, would set about to describe the relevant conduct if *they* had started from scratch.[18]

This is not that surprising, and it seems like everyone is on board with using the singular *they*. In 2016, the American Dialect Society, whose membership includes linguists, grammarians, writers, and editors, selected the neutral singular *they* as Word of the Year.[19] Further, other style guides, such as the *Chicago Manual of Style*, and the Associated Press, recognized *they* as a singular pronoun in 2017. Similarly, *Dreyer's English* states that the singular *they* is "not the wave of the future; it's the wave of the present."[20]

Experts in legal writing have also joined the chorus. In her comprehensive article, *Get with the Pronoun*, legal writing director at Brooklyn Law School, Heidi Brown, referring to *they*, stated that it "packs enough power to foster clarity, accuracy, inclusion, and respect in legal writing."[21] Another professor of legal writing and his co-author, a Michigan Supreme Court staff attorney, pointed out that "[m]ore and more writing experts and guides... are trumpeting that the once-plural-only pronoun may now be used as a singular pronoun...."[22] And legal writing director at the University of Arizona College of Law, Susie Salmon, proclaimed, "*They* is now a singular, gender-neutral pronoun. Maybe we should accept it and move on with our lives."[23]

Not everyone, however, has moved on with their lives, and there are some experts who believe that instead of always using *they* as a singular pronoun, sometimes the better strategy is to rewrite the sentence to avoid the issue. Let's look at some general style guides first. Author of *Grammar Girl*, Mignon Fogarty, believes that "someday *they* will be the

---

18. *Id.* at 357.
19. Brown, *supra* note 2, at 69, 69 n.38.
20. Benjamin Dreyer, Dreyer's English 93 (2019).
21. Brown, *supra* note 2, at 61.
22. Brad Charles & Thomas Myers, *Evolving* They, Mich. Bar J., June 2019, at 38, 38.
23. Susie Salmon, *Them!*, Ariz. Att'y, Oct. 2018, at 10, 10.

acceptable choice."[24] She refers to credible references that will back you up for using *they* with a singular antecedent, such as *Random House Dictionary* and *Fowler's Modern English Usage*. She also includes this warning: "if you are responsible to superiors, there's a good chance that at least one of them will think you are careless or ignorant if you use *they* with a singular antecedent."[25] In that case, she recommends rewriting the sentence to avoid the problem. And the Associated Press, which authorized journalists to use the singular *they* in 2017, nonetheless indicated a preference for grammatical workarounds.[26]

Similarly, some legal writing experts suggest a workaround. The *Redbook* has a lengthy explanation of the issue but provides this statistic: Despite "the official approval in some style manuals of the singular *they*, a 2018 poll found that half of American readers consider it objectionable. So be forewarned."[27] Accordingly, that guide recommends avoiding the issue by achieving "invisible gender-neutrality" as the best course of action. Similarly, while expert Wayne Schiess acknowledged that many are already using the singular *they* and suggested that one option is to just jump on the bandwagon, he added that another option, in formal legal writing, is to "write around the problem."[28] Finally, in the Idaho State

---

24. MIGNON FOGARTY, GRAMMAR GIRL'S QUICK AND DIRTY TIPS FOR BETTER WRITING 61 (2008).

25. *Id.* Fogarty's new guide in 2019 for students includes this same advice. *Compare id., with* MIGNON FOGARTY, GRAMMAR GIRL PRESENTS THE ULTIMATE WRITING GUIDE FOR STUDENTS 30–31 (2d ed. 2019).

26. Brown, *supra* note 2, at 69.

27. REDBOOK, *supra* note 1, at 204. The *Redbook* does not say what poll it is referring to. In a Pew Research Center survey conducted in fall 2018, roughly half of Americans say they would be somewhat or very comfortable using a gender-neutral pronoun, while 47% say they would be somewhat or very uncomfortable doing so. Notable differences exist based on age and political party. A.W. Geiger & Nikki Graff, *About One-in-Five U.S. Adults Know Someone Who Goes by a Gender-Neutral Pronoun*, PEW RSCH. CTR. (Sept. 5, 2019) https://www.pewresearch.org/fact-tank/2019/09/05/gender-neutral-pronouns/. In *Get with the Pronoun*, Brown, focusing on Gen Z'ers, discussed a survey where 56% of that population says they know someone who uses gender-neutral pronouns. Brown, *supra* note 2, at 63.

28. Wayne Schiess, *Singular "They"*, UNIV. TEX. AUSTIN BLOG SERV.: LEGIBLE (Dec. 9, 2019), https://sites.utexas.edu/legalwriting/2019/12/09/singular-they/.

Bar *Advocate*, a legal writing professor mentioned that while using *they* is commonplace, "[m]any legal readers... are still jarred by its usage."[29]

How do you write "around" the problem? Let's take our law student example above:

> Sentence with they as singular pronoun: A law *student* might not take legal writing if *they* find out the class starts at 8:00 a.m.

> Workaround that avoids the issue: Law students might not take legal writing if *they* find out the class starts at 8:00 a.m.

All that was required was to turn the singular noun "law student" into a plural noun, so that *they* matches the plural noun.

Here's one more example:

> Sentence with they as singular pronoun: A dog owner must make sure their dog gets a rabies shot once every three years.

> Workaround that avoids the issue: Dog owners must make sure their dogs get a rabies shot once every three years.

As with all style issues, pay attention to your audience.

D. Situations Where "They" Should Be Avoided

In addition, there are situations where *they* is simply not the right pronoun to use. Because I have seen students misuse *they* in these situations, I want to make sure you don't make these same mistakes.

First, do not use *they* when the resulting meaning would be ambiguous. Take the following sentence:

> Defendant cooperated with the arresting police officers and disclosed *they* were in possession of drugs.

In this sentence, does *they* refer to the defendant or to the arresting police officers? Because you cannot tell, there is an ambiguity, so you need to rewrite the sentence.

---

29. Tenielle Fordyce-Ruff, *Fairness, Clarity, Precision, and Reaction: Gender-Free and Bias-Free Word Choice*, ADVOCATE, Aug. 2015, at 52, 52 n.2.

Ex: Defendant cooperated and admitted to being in possession of drugs.

Because of this potential for ambiguity, be on the lookout, especially when *they* follows two or more people or things.[30]

Indeed, this type of ambiguity sparked litigation in Michigan over the interpretation of an ordinance.[31] In that case, the plaintiffs owned land zoned for agricultural-residential use and wanted to build a mobile home park. The applicable ordinance provided that "[m]obile homes are permitted in Mobile Home Parks. They shall be permitted in Mobile Home Subdivision and Residential-Agricultural Districts, if at a minimum, the conditions... are met." The plaintiffs interpreted the ordinance as permitting mobile home *parks* in agricultural-residential districts, arguing that "they" refers to mobile home parks. The defendant disagreed, interpreting the same words as permitting mobile homes in agricultural-residential districts because *they* referred to mobile homes, not mobile home parks. The court agreed with the defendant,[32] but the point is the imprecise use of the pronoun *they* created ambiguity, which led to litigation.

Another time you should not use *they* is to describe a known person if that person has not indicated that they want to be called *they*. Let's say Justin Timberlake gets sued and is now a defendant in a lawsuit. How would you refer to him?

Defendant (referring to Justin Timberlake) testified that *he* wrote the song lyrics without input from Plaintiff.

In other words, it's important for you to respect an individual's wishes when it comes to pronouns.

---

30. Charles & Myers, *supra* note 22, at 39.

31. Lamotte Coach Light Corp. v. Twp. of Lamotte, No. 240907, 2003 WL 22339169, at *1 (Mich. Ct. App. Oct. 14, 2003) (per curiam).

32. *Id.* at *2.

E. The Non-Binary or Transgender Client

What if you represent a client who uses gender-neutral pronouns or is transgender and uses pronouns that are different from their sex assigned at birth? One sound recommendation is to talk through the risks with your client, including the risk of a potentially unfriendly audience (such as a court) before using *they*. You could elect to use the pronoun, and then "respectfully yet firmly educate a reader who might be unfamiliar with a particular grammatical structure."[33] For example, in *Bostock v. Clayton Cnty.*,[34] attorneys for Aimee Stephens, one of the plaintiffs, described her as follows in the introduction:

> Aimee Stephens was fired from her position as funeral director and embalmer because of her employer's stereotypes about how women and men should appear and behave. Ms. Stephens was assigned a male gender at birth and initially presented in a stereotypically masculine way at work, although she has known that she is female for most of her life.[35]

The lawyers then placed this additional information in a footnote: "To be transgender is to have a gender identity different from one's assigned sex at birth."[36] Through their writing, the lawyers for Ms. Stephens educated the Court in a respectful and straightforward way.

It is widely accepted in legal writing that in these situations, using gender-appropriate pronouns is the norm. Indeed, the U.S. Supreme Court used gender-appropriate language when referring to Ms. Stephens in its opinion. The Court held that Title VII's prohibition against sex discrimination in employment applies to both gay and transgender individuals.[37] Writing about Aimee Stephens, the Court explained that she presented as a male when she first started working at a funeral home.[38] After working there for six years, she wrote a letter to her employer explaining that she planned to "live and work fulltime as a

---

33. Brown, *supra* note 2, at 73.

34. 140 S.Ct. 1731 (2020).

35. Brief for Respondent Aimee Stephens at 1, Bostock v. Clayton Cnty., 140 S. Ct. 1731 (2020) (No. 18-107), 2018 WL 5308150, at *1.

36. *Id.* at *1 n.1.

37. *Bostock*, 140 S. Ct. at 1737.

38. *Id.* at 1738.

woman" after she returned from an upcoming vacation, prompting the funeral home to fire her. Throughout its opinion, the Supreme Court referred to Stephens as "her" or "she."

The rule is simple and bears restating: If you know a party's pronouns, use them. And do the work to consult with and educate your client.

For their part, most of the federal appellate courts have employed gender-appropriate language,[39] but there are notable exceptions. For example, in *United States v. Thomason*,[40] the defendant appealed their sentence based on prosecutorial misconduct because the prosecutor used masculine pronouns and labels at trial, ignoring their preference for using *they*, *them*, or *their*.[41] Even though the United States Attorney's Office referred to the defendant as *they* in its brief, the Eighth Circuit instead used the pronouns *he* or *him* when referring to the defendant throughout its opinion.[42] The Fifth Circuit has also refused to honor a party's request to use a specific set of pronouns.[43]

In conclusion, some of the rules for pronouns are clear, and you should follow them. Others, however, have the potential to make some readers raise their eyebrows, so consider your audience, whether that may be your writing professor, your supervisor, your client, or a court. And when you walk into a bar, make your life simple by ordering your own drink.

---

39. Chan Tov McNamarah, *Some Notes on Courts and Courtesy*, 107 Va. L. Rev. Online 317, 320 n. 10 (Dec. 2021) (see collection of cases from the Third, Fourth, Seventh, Tenth, and Eleventh Circuits).

40. 991 F.3d 910 (8th Cir. 2021).

41. *Id.* at 914.

42. *Compare* Brief of Appellee, *Thomason*, 991 F.3d 910 (No. 19-2537), 2020 WL 4354459, *with Thomason*, 991 F.3d 910.

43. United States v. Varner, 948 F.3d 250, 256 (5th Cir. 2020) (using *he* to refer to plaintiff Kathrine Nicole Jett, stating that using gender-appropriate language would give the impression of wrongful partiality towards Jett).

Lowercase, Uppercase, and CamelCase

. . . .

I know that title caught your attention because most likely, you have no idea what CamelCase is. Read on. I do not want to take the mystery out of the term right off the bat. This chapter is about capitalization, a close cousin of grammar and punctuation; like mistakes in grammar and punctuation, if you capitalize words incorrectly, that could leave a negative impression with your reader.[1] In this chapter, after a brief history lesson on capitalization, you will learn about trends in capitalization generally, views of capitalization in legal writing, and guidelines for capitalization focusing on the most common issues you will face in legal writing.

A. Shortest Ever History Lesson

You already know that uppercase letters are capitals (also called "majuscule" letters, if you want to impress your friends), and lowercase letters are small letters (also called "minuscule" letters).[2] Have you ever wondered how they got these names? Historians believe that capital let-

---

1. John M. Keating, *Confident Capitals—Tips on Capitalization in Legal Writing*, N.J. LAW., Oct. 2020, at 12, 13 ("Mastering and integrating capitalization style will increase clarity and consistency in legal writing.").

2. *Why Are There Uppercase and Lowercase Letters?*, WONDEROPOLIS, http://wonderopolis.org/wonder/why-are-there-uppercase-and-lowercase-letters (last visited Mar. 17, 2022); *Why Do We Use Uppercase and Lowercase Letters?*, DICTIONARY.COM (July 24, 2020), https://www.dictionary.com/e/capitals.

ters were invented first, and the first alphabets were written in all capital letters. Then, lowercase letters were invented, making writing easier to read. The terms "uppercase" and "lowercase" are derived from where printers kept the metal pieces used to print the letters long ago. The letters were kept in boxes called cases. The smaller letters were kept in a lower box that was easier for printers to reach because they were used more often, while the bigger letters were kept in a higher box. The terms "uppercase" and "lowercase" started to be used in the 1700s, and there were no rules for capitalization in English until this period.[3]

B. Capitalization Trends

Just like fashion trends, capitalization trends come and go. Let's look at the Declaration of Independence and the book *Winnie the Pooh*. In 1776, when the Declaration of Independence was written, British capitalization rules were still dominant in America, and there was a trend toward using a lot of capitalization.[4] That's why you see some odd capitalization choices in it, as this passage shows:

> We hold these truths to be self-evident, that all men... are endowed... with certain unalienable Rights, that among these are Life, Liberty and the pursuit of Happiness.—That to secure these rights, Governments are instituted among Men, deriving their just powers from the consent of the governed,—That whenever any Form of Government becomes destructive of these ends, it is the Right of the People to... institute new Government,... organizing its powers in such form, as to them shall seem most likely to effect their Safety and Happiness.[5]

Notice that "Rights," "Life," "Liberty" "Happiness," "Governments," "Men," "Form," "People," and "Safety," are all capitalized even though today, you would use lowercase.

---

3. DICTIONARY.COM, *supra* note 2.

4. *See Independence Day (The Language of the Declaration of Independence)*, PROOFED (July 2, 2016), https://getproofed.com/writing-tips/language-of-the-declaration-of-inde pendence/.

5. THE DECLARATION OF INDEPENDENCE para. 2 (U.S. 1776).

About 150 years later, *Winnie the Pooh* was published,[6] and, even then, you see some odd capitalization choices, such as referring to Winnie the Pooh as the "Bear of Very Little Brain."[7]

Moving forward in time, *The Redbook*, a legal style guide last published in 2018, advises legal writers to follow the modern trend towards less capitalization.[8] But writers in general, who apparently long for the old days, are now opting for more capitalization.[9] Why is this? One theory—which makes perfect sense—is the dramatic uptick in how much people communicate these days by text and Twitter.[10] Neither text messaging nor Twitter have simple, built-in mechanisms for emphasizing words using italics or bold face, so that leaves writers with no option but to capitalize words (which can be done easily) for emphasis. Another cause is the competitive nature of these forms of social media—everyone is clamoring for attention and using capital letters is one way to get it.[11]

The problem is that this trend is now showing up in other kinds of writing, including legal writing, so we need to reverse it.

---

6. A. A. Milne, Winnie-the-Pooh iv (Egmont UK Ltd., 2004).

7. *Id.* at 45; James Harbeck, *The New Rules of Capitalization*, The Week (May 29, 2018), https://theweek.com/articles/773679/new-rules-capitalization.

8. Bryan A. Garner, The Redbook: A Manual on Legal Style 67 (4th ed. 2018) [hereinafter Redbook] ("Use lowercase unless a rule calls for capitalization.").

9. *See* Katy Waldman, *The Digital Epidemic of Random Midsentence Capitalization*, Slate (Aug. 25, 2016, 9:15 AM), https://slate.com/technology/2016/08/why-does-the-inter net-insert-random-capital-letters-into-the-middle-of-sentences.html; Harbeck, *supra* note 7; Nicole Galluci, *A Look at the Ubiquitous Habit of Capitalizing Letters to Make a Point*, Mashable Se. Asia (June 19, 2019), https://mashable.com/article/capitaliing-first-letter -words-trend.

10. *E.g.*, Waldman, *supra* note 9; Galluci, *supra* note 9.

11. Gallucci, *supra* note 9.

C. Legal Writing Views

Most legal writing experts, including judges, complain about too much capitalizing in legal writing. For example, Judge Lebovits called capitalizing incorrectly a "Capital Offense," and recommended "downsizing."[12]

Similarly, the Seventh Circuit issued guidelines for briefs and other papers, suggesting that lawyers "[a]void setting text in all caps."[13] The court explained why all-caps text should be avoided:

> All-caps text [when referring to party names] attracts the eye (so does boldface) and makes it harder to read what is in between—yet what lies between the parties' names is exactly what you want the judge to read. All-caps text in outlines and section captions also is hard to read, even worse than underlining. Capitals all are rectangular, so the reader can't use shapes (including ascenders and descenders) as cues. Underlined, all caps, boldface text is almost illegible.[14]

Therefore, no one should be left to wonder what the Seventh Circuit thinks about capitalizing too much.

Similarly, Judge Kressel, a federal bankruptcy judge, after years of waiting in vain for lawyers to take a hint from his edits to their proposed orders, issued guidelines telling them to stop using so much capitalization.[15] In guideline six, the judge criticized lawyers because they were too fond of capitalization:

> Lawyers apparently love to capitalize words. Pleadings, including proposed orders, are commonly full of words that are capi-

---

12. Gerald Lebovits, *Uppercasing Needn't Be a Capital Crime*, N.Y. St. Bar Ass'n J., May 2003, at 64, 64, 61.

13. Requirements and Suggestions for Typography in Briefs and Other Papers, U.S. Ct. of App. for the Seventh Cir. 6 (n.d.).

14. *Id.*

15. Debra Cassens Weiss, *Judge Orders Lawyers to Stop Using Capitalization 'With Abandon,'* ABA J. (Dec. 14, 2009, 3:31 PM), https://www.abajournal.com/news/article/bankruptcy_judge_orders_lawyers_to_stop_using_capitalization_with_abandon; *see also* Robert J. Kressel, *Save the Adverb*, Ill. St. Bar Ass'n: Bench & Bar, Apr. 2010, at 5, 5–6.

talized, not quite randomly, but certainly with great abandon. Please limit the use of capitalization to proper names. For example, do not capitalize court, motion, movant, debtor, trustee, order, affidavit, stipulation, mortgage, lease or any of the other numerous words that are commonly capitalized.[16]

Legal writing experts generally agree that lawyers are too fond of capitalization. Expert Bryan Garner, listing the twenty most common sentence-level faults among legal writers, included overcapitalization as one fault.[17] Similarly, one lawyer, providing tips on capitalization, identified three common sources of confusion about capitalization in legal writing: party designations, titles of court documents, and the word "court."[18] Writing in the *Minnesota Lawyer*, another lawyer opined that "[y]oung lawyers in particular, and legal administrative assistants seem to have a passion for capitalizing anything that refers to a court or a pleading. But that is not what the *Bluebook* says, and it does not make much sense."[19] Finally, a legal writing professor also noticed that her students' "capitalization of certain words was wildly inconsistent" and they needed help.[20] Because both students and lawyers need help with capitalization, legal writing blogs are also sprinkled with advice on the topic.[21]

---

16. Kressel, *supra* note 15, at 5.

17. Bryan A. Garner, *The 20 Most Common Sentence-Level Faults Among Legal Writers*, MICH. BAR J., Feb. 2012, at 48, 48.

18. Keating, *supra* note 1, at 13.

19. Eric J. Magnuson & Lisa Beane, *How Not to Yell at the Court*, LEGAL NEWS, Feb. 18, 2019, 2019 WLNR 4847230.

20. Laura Graham, *Capitalization for Practitioners: Consistency Counts!*, N.C. BAR ASS'N (Jan. 1, 2015), https://www.ncbar.org/news/capitalization-for-practitioners-consistency-counts/.

21. E.g., Ross Guberman, *Four Motion Mistakes*, LEGAL WRITING PRO, https://www.legalwritingpro.com/articles/four-motion-mistakes/ (last visited Mar. 18, 2022); Savannah Blackwell, *Legal Writing Tip: Know When to Capitalize the "C" in Court* (Oct. 23, 2018), https://www.sfbar.org/blog/legal-writing-tip-know-when-to-capitalize-the-c-in-court/.

D. Key Capitalization Issues

Let's get to the key rules.[22] First, we will cover the four most common mistakes that lawyers (and students) make: capitalization of the word "court," capitalization of the names of parties, capitalization of names of documents filed with the court, and capitalization of headings in briefs. Then, we will cover important capitalization rules surrounding other phrases that you will use in legal writing (although not as frequently).

E. Capitalization of "Court"

It is somewhat ironic that lawyers, including those who regularly appear before a court, struggle with when to capitalize the word "court." The legal citation guides agree on three situations when you must capitalize the word "court": (1) when referring to the United States Supreme Court; (2) when using the full name of any court; and (3) when referring to the court you are before, no matter the level of that court.[23] They also agree that you should capitalize the name of a circuit court but only when you are referring to it by number, such as "the Seventh Circuit" but not when you are writing, "The circuit court held."

The *Redbook* adds to this list of categories, instructing writers to also capitalize, "the highest tribunal in the jurisdiction whose laws govern the outcome, such as a state supreme court."[24]

Let's go back to the above list and provide some examples. For the United States Supreme Court, you would capitalize the word "court," whether you are spelling out the court's name in full or not:

---

22. If you want to figure out the rule on every issue you might encounter, you can consult the *Bluebook*, the *ALWD Guide*, and the *Redbook*, but even they cannot cover every issue you might encounter. For that reason, *ALWD* and *Bluebook* suggest you refer to style manuals such as the *U.S. Government Publishing Office Style Manual*, the *Redbook*, or *The Chicago Manual of Style* if there is no rule on point in these guides. THE BLUEBOOK: A UNIFORM SYSTEM OF CITATION R. 8(c), at 92 (Columbia L. Rev. Ass'n et al. eds, 21st ed. 2020) [hereinafter Bluebook]; CAROLYN V. WILLIAMS, ASS'N OF LEGAL WRITING DIRS., ALWD GUIDE TO LEGAL CITATION 14 (Wolters Kluwer 7th ed.) [hereinafter ALWD].

23. ALWD, *supra* note 22, at 15; BLUEBOOK, *supra* note 22, at 10.

24. REDBOOK, *supra* note 8, at 76.

Example: The United States Supreme Court held that Title VII applied.

Example: The Court held that Title VII applied.

When spelling out the full name of any court, you capitalize the words, like this:

Example: The Ohio Supreme Court has held....

Under the *Redbook*'s rule, you would also capitalize the C in court if you were appearing in a case in which Ohio law governed the outcome, and you were referring to the Ohio Supreme Court, even if you did not spell out the name of the court in full:[25]

Example: The Court [referring to the Ohio Supreme Court] has held that the one-year statute of limitations governs cases involving a public entity.

The final time you capitalize the *c* in *court* is when you are referring to the court you are appearing before:

Example: For the reasons stated in this brief, the Court should grant the motion for summary judgment.

But what if you are not writing to a court directly but instead writing an office memorandum for in-house use only? How do you capitalize the word court in that document? The *Bluebook* doesn't offer any guidance, and the *ALWD Guide* seems to indicate that you would not capitalize "court" because in listing the types of documents where you capitalize the *c*, it only includes documents filed with a court, such as a complaint, a motion, or a brief.[26]

---

25. *Id.* at 76. The Redbook's rule is consistent with at least one state's local rules. In California, the style manual provides that lawyers must "always capitalize partial names when describing the Supreme Court of California (e.g., the Supreme Court) or one of the California Courts of Appeal (e.g., the Court of Appeal, Fourth District, Division Two). Edward W. Jessen, California Style Manual § 4:1, at 116. (4th ed. 2000). The *Redbook* rule is also consistent with the capitalization rule on referring to the U.S. Supreme Court (capitalize the term whether you are spelling it out in full or not).

26. ALWD, *supra* note 22, at 15.

In my (maybe not so humble) opinion, memos should *not* be excluded from the types of documents where you should capitalize the *c* in *court* if warranted. After all, in many situations, lawyers are going to take that memo and turn it into a brief to be filed with a court, and it will save time if the capitalization is already correctly done.

Finally, as with all advice on style, pay attention to your local rules and your audience. For example, if you are practicing in California, the California Style Manual specifically instructs lawyers to capitalize the official name of the California Supreme Court whether your reference is in full or only partial.[27]

F. Capitalization of Parties

The second issue lawyers (and law students) struggle with is when to capitalize party designations, such as plaintiff or defendant. Only capitalize the first letter of a party designation when you are using it to substitute for a party name in *your* case.[28] Here is an example:

> Example: Defendant [referring to the defendant in *your* case] testified that he ran through a red light.

Do not capitalize the first letter of *defendant* or *plaintiff* (or similar designation) if you are referring to a party other than the case before the court. For example, if you are talking about another case where the defendant in that case ran a red light, you would write this:

> Example: In *Smith*, the court held that the defendant was negligent where he ran a red light.

Because you are substituting the word "Defendant" for the name of a party, the best practice is to eliminate the article "the" before the word "Defendant."[29]

Despite the above, ideally, you should eliminate references such as Plaintiff and Defendant in your case and call parties by their names in-

---

27. *See* Jessen, *supra* note 25, at 116.

28. Bluebook, *supra* note 22, at 10, ALWD, *supra* note 22, at 15.

29. Ross Guberman, *Capitalization Cheat Sheet*, Legal Writing Pro (2007), https://legalwritingpro.com/pdf/capitalization.pdf.

stead.[30] This is another time to make sure to follow the court rules that apply specifically to your case. For example, Rule 28(d) of the Federal Rules of Appellate Procedure provides that "counsel should minimize use of the terms 'appellant' and 'appellee.' To make briefs clear, counsel should use the parties' actual names or the designations used in the lower court or agency proceeding, or such descriptive terms as 'the employee,' 'the injured person,' 'the taxpayer,' 'the ship,' 'the stevedore.'"[31] Thus, the use of the names of parties, or a descriptor such as "employee" or "employer," will enhance clarity.

G. Capitalization of Names of Documents

Next, we will cover how to capitalize the names of court documents filed in a case. The convention is to capitalize the name of a document only when: (1) it is a document filed in your case; and (2) the reference is to the actual title or a shortened form.[32] Similar to the rule for capitalizing party designations, you would not capitalize it if you were using the name or type of a document generically:

> Example: On December 19, 2021, Defendant filed a Motion for Partial Summary Judgment on the Issue of Punitive Damages.

> Example: On December 19, 2021, Defendant filed a motion for partial summary judgment relating to punitive damages.

> Example: Defendant filed its motion after the deadline the Court set in this case.

Again, despite these capitalization rules, there is usually no reason to spell out the title of a filed document by its full name. It usually promotes brevity (without sacrificing clarity, unless several motions to dismiss have been filed) to use a shorthand instead.[33] Therefore, instead of

---

30. REDBOOK, *supra* note 8, at 78.

31. FED. R. APP. P. 28(d). The California Style Manual has a similar provision: "In briefs and opinions, generally use the trial designations or personal names in referring to the parties (i.e., do not use 'Appellant' and "Respondent')." JESSEN, *supra* note 25, at 220.

32. BLUEBOOK, *supra* note 22, at 10; *see* Guberman, *supra* note 21.

33. Magnuson & Beane, *supra* note 19.

writing, "Plaintiff's Motion to Dismiss Complaint for Failure to State a Claim," you can write, "Plaintiff's motion to dismiss…."

H. Capitalization of Headings

The final issue that many practitioners (and law students) struggle with is how to capitalize either main section headings or point headings. First, let's get our terminology straight. A "main" section heading, or short, "top-level heading" is a short phrase of no more than one line. Examples are titles, such as, "Argument," "Conclusion," "Statement of Facts," or "Introduction." For those types of headings, it is appropriate to use all capital letters and boldface.[34]

For point headings, that is, headings and subheadings that are *not* main section headings, *avoid* using all capital letters because that will make them difficult to read. In fact, psychologists have concluded that using all capital letters in a heading *decreases* the speed of reading as compared to lowercase letters.[35] In repeated tests on adults, the studies showed that all capital letters decreased the reading time by 9.5% to 19%. The other problem with using all capital letters is that it is like shouting at the court,[36] and courts do not appreciate that. Further, if you use all capital letters, it could signal to your reader that your style is outdated.[37]

For its part, the Seventh Circuit has issued its own guidelines on headings, emphasizing that when headings are set in all capital letters, they can be "very hard to follow."[38] It then gives both "good" and "bad" examples of heading styles, showing that the heading using all caps is harder to read.

34. REDBOOK, *supra* note 8, at 106.

35. Ruth Anne Robbins, *Painting with Print: Incorporating Concepts of Typographic and Layout Design into the Text of Legal Writing Documents*, 2 LEGAL COMM. & RHETORIC: JALWD 108, 115 (2004); Miles A. Tinker, *Prolonged Reading Tasks in Visual Research*, 39 J. APPLIED PSYCH. 444, 444, 446 (1955).

36. Magnuson & Beane, *supra* note 19.

37. *See* Goerge Khoury, *When Pleading Do You Write plaintiff, Plaintiff, or PLAINTIFF*, FINDLAW (July 21, 2017, 7:00 AM), https://www.findlaw.com/legalblogs/strategist/when-pleading-do-you-write-plaintiff-plaintiff-or-plaintiff/.

38. U.S. CT. OF APP. FOR THE SEVENTH CIR., *supra* note 13, at 6–7.

The U.S. Solicitor General's Office, however, has its own capitalization style, proving once again that if your employer does it a certain way, follow those conventions. In its brief filed with the U.S. Supreme Court in *Federal Election Commission v. Ted Cruz for Senate*, where there were three levels of headings, the headings were written using three levels of capitalization—all capital letters, initial capital letters only,[39] and lowercase sentence style:

I. APPELLEES LACK ARTICLE III STANDING

   A. Appellees' Injury Is Not Traceable To, And Would Not Be Redressed By Restraining The Enforcement Of, BCRA's Loan-Repayment Limit

      1. *Appellees have not shown that their injury is fairly traceable to BCRA's loan-repayment limit or that restraining its enforcement would redress the injury*

      2. *An FEC regulation currently precludes the committee from repaying the remaining $10,000 of Senator Cruz's loan, but that regulatory bar does not give appellees standing to challenge the statutory loan-repayment limit* [40]

Besides using all capital letters for the first heading, look closely—though all the headings but the first-level heading form a complete sentence, no periods appear at the end of the sentences. I was curious why the office followed this practice, so I did what any rational person would do—I reached out to a former member of the Solicitor General's Office to ask why. I learned that this has been the way the Solicitor General's Office has capitalized headings for a long time. The possible reason for the lack of periods is that the headings do not always form complete

---

39. When you capitalize main words in a heading and leave other words in lowercase, you might have questions on whether to capitalize a word or not. The *Redbook* says not to capitalize articles, such as "the" or "a," a conjunction or preposition shorter than five letters, or the word "to" used in an infinitive. REDBOOK, *supra* note 8, at 73.

40. Brief for the Fed. Election Comm'n at 10–12, 16, Fed. Election Comm'n v. Ted Cruz for Senate, 142 S. Ct. 55 (2021) (No. 21-12).

sentences, so dropping periods for all headings is more consistent. Some also view it as "cleaner" and "more aesthetically pleasing."[41]

Interestingly, on the period question, Bryan Garner seems to disagree, for in response to a Tweet asking whether you put a period at the end of a heading in a brief or motion, he responded, "Yes. Point headings are complete sentences, and they end with periods."[42]

Moral of the story: follow best practices, but follow the rules and conventions that govern your situation.

I. Other Situations

Next, we are going to turn to some additional rules that you will also find helpful. Unlike the issues covered above, which tend to arise in virtually every paper you file with a court, the issues below tend to arise less frequently.

1. Capitalization of Proper Noun but Not the Adjective

Lawyers often refer to nouns such as Congress or the U.S. Constitution. Those terms should be capitalized. But a derivative of those words used as an adjective (as opposed to a proper noun) is *not* capitalized. Therefore, if you write, "She claims the police violated her constitutional rights," you do not capitalize the *c* in *constitutional*. Or, if you write, "It was time for congressional action," you do not capitalize the *c* in *congressional*.[43]

2. Capitalization of Titles

Let's cover two kinds of titles that students often write about: job titles and statutory titles. On job titles, you should capitalize a title that follows a person's name or substitutes for a name only if the title identifies a VIP

---

41. E-mail from Jeffrey B. Wall to author (Jan. 14, 2022) (on file with author).

42. Bryan A. Garner (@BryanAGarner), TWITTER (March 15, 2016), https://twitter.com/bryanagarner/status/709781537089265666?lang=en.

43. REDBOOK, *supra* note 8, at 72. Adjectives derived from words that exist *only* as proper nouns, however, should generally still be capitalized: for example, American from America. *Id.*

who you are unlikely to grab a cup of coffee with—a head or assistant head of state, a diplomatic title, a ruler, or royalty, like this: "Boris Johnson, Prime Minister of England." Do not, however, capitalize titles that do not fall into these categories, and do not capitalize job descriptions, even when used before names. Here are examples:

> Jack Reed, senator from Rhode Island
> Steve Kerr, coach of the Golden State Warriors
> Tim Cook, president of Apple
> The basketball player Stephen Curry

Now that you understand that rule, let's move on to statutes. You should capitalize the name of a statute in two situations—if you are naming the act in full or if you are using a shorthand for that same statute after spelling it out in full once.[44] For example, let's say you are referring to the Uniform Trade Secrets Act, and you capitalize those words. Then, after that first reference, you use a shorthand, such as Act. You capitalize the *A* in *Act*. However, if you are not using a statutory reference as a proper noun, you do not capitalize it, such as in this example:

> Eleven states have passed a trade secrets act.

3. Defined Terms and Acronyms

The last topic I want to cover is capitalization of defined terms and acronyms. In many situations, lawyers will use a defined term to refer to either a party or other item. In that situation, the defined term is capitalized.[45] For example, let's say you are explaining a situation where the parties entered into two different contracts, and you want to talk about both, so you do this:

> On June 1, 2021, the parties entered into a Contract for the Sale of 2020 North 22nd Avenue ("Contract One"), and, a month later, the parties entered into a Contract for the Sale of 2323 East End Avenue ("Contract Two"). Discussions sur-

---

44. Redbook, *supra* note 8, at 70.
45. ALWD, *supra* note 22, at 13.

rounding Contract One were between Glacier and James Delbert.

Notice how you capitalize the shorthand reference to both Contract One and Contract Two.

Turning to acronyms, you should capitalize all of the letters, unless an exception applies. For example, you would want to capitalize NAACP, NBA, EPA, ACLU, or NATO. But some common acronyms do not use all caps, such as Nasdaq. In general, if you are unsure, respect institutional preferences (look up how the institution refers to itself)[46] and/or consult a dictionary.

"Have I got a great idea for you."

---

46. REDBOOK, *supra* note 8, at 75.

J. CamelCase

And now, we are turning to what you have all been waiting for: CamelCase. CamelCase is when a capital letter is used for the first letter of a word forming the second element of a closed compound.[47] Because that's a mouthful, it's much easier to give you examples, such as PayPal, MasterCard, iPhone, and eBay. Whoever named it CamelCase is a genius because if you think about a camel and its hump right in the middle, that's what is happening with these words—the capital letter is a hump in the middle. In a hypothetical case my students wrote about recently, the focus of the hypothetical was on whether the First Amendment prevented a public employee from getting fired for speaking out against the employee's employer in a WhatsApp message. Students then had to use CamelCase every time they referred to the message, so there will be times you will use CamelCase in legal writing. Next time you ride a camel, I know you will be thinking about this form of capitalization.

In conclusion, the current trend is not to supersize but to downsize, or to Marie Kondo your capital letters. Having said that, the rules and conventions governing your situation always control. Therefore, if your writing professor tells you, "Use all capital letters in all headings," do that. After all, the last person you want to argue with is your writing professor.

---

47. *Camel case*, WIKIPEDIA, https://en.wikipedia.org/wiki/Camel_case (last visited Mar. 18, 2022).

Smart, Single, Ambidextrous...
and Looking to Pair Up
Quotations

. . . .

For a second, you might have thought you wandered onto a dating app. But alas, this book is about legal writing, and this chapter is about all issues pertaining to quotations. I know that at least some of you are thinking, I know what a quotation is; tell me something I do not know. (Notice I did not use quotation marks around what I think are your thoughts because they are unnecessary.[1])

In this chapter, we will cover when and when not to quote, different uses of quotations, how to introduce quotations, and the details surrounding quotations—such as the type of quotation marks, the use of ellipses, the use of brackets, and the placement of punctuation with quotation marks. Finally, we will cover a new trend in legal writing called "cleaned-up" quotations[2] (which does not refer to cleaning up inappropriate language).

---

1. BENJAMIN DREYER, DREYER'S ENGLISH 51–52 (2019) (explaining that "articulated rumination" does not need to be encased in quotation marks because this is not actual dialogue).

2. Note that some writers put hyphens in between cleaned and up when appearing before the word "quotations." The Redbook does use a hyphen. BRYAN A. GARNER, THE REDBOOK: A MANUAL ON LEGAL STYLE 159 (4th ed. 2018) [hereinafter REDBOOK]. However, the *ALWD Guide to Legal Citation* does not. CAROLYN V. WILLIAMS, ASS'N OF LEGAL WRITING DIRS., ALWD GUIDE TO LEGAL CITATION 406 (Wolters Kluwer 7th ed.) [hereinafter ALWD]. This is just another example where people cannot agree on hyphen usage. *See* Chapter 6 on hyphens, em dashes, and en dashes.

A. One Rule of Thumb: Do Not Overquote

Your first challenge is to figure out if you should quote or not. You might be better off paraphrasing instead because if your brief consists of nothing more than back-to-back quotations, your reader will assume that you have not undertaken a thorough analysis of the argument and have nothing to add.[3] This is especially true for beginning law students, who incorrectly assume that courts always know the best way to word something. But reading and interpreting a case should not be a passive activity; students need to be "willing to take on the texts rather than just take them in."[4]

Paraphrasing means taking what a court has to say and putting it into your own words. Because you are incorporating a court's ideas (usually), you still need to include authority supporting your paraphrase. When paraphrasing, you can improve on the clarity of the original text, make it more concise, and tie it more effectively into your case.[5] Therefore, if you write a brief and it consists of nothing more than quotation after quotation, something is wrong.

Keep in mind that this view of overquoting is not mine alone: the experts agree. Let us begin with what judges think because, after all, they decide what happens in your case, so their views matter. In a survey of more than a thousand state and federal judges, they indicated their strong disapproval of block quotations[6]—which are quotations of more than 50 words that are indented on a page. If information is presented in a block quotation, judges say they may skip the quotation entirely. One judge said, "Do not block quote more than three lines. After that, I may stop reading," and another judge stressed his disdain for block quotations in even stronger words: "Huge block quotes are terrible. It's much more persuasive to paraphrase the reasoning and then quote only the

---

3. *See, e.g.*, Marc A. Grinker, *Quotation Incorporation*, Chicago–Kent Coll. of L.: The L. Student's Guide to Legal Writing (1994), http://www.kentlaw.edu/academics/lrw/grinker/LwtaQuotation_Incorporation.htm; Rebekah Hanley, *When and How to Borrow Language*, Or. St. Bar Bull., Feb.–Mar. 2011, at 13, 13.

4. Elizabeth Fajans & Mary R. Falk, *Against the Tyranny of Paraphrase: Talking Back to Texts*, 78 Cornell L. Rev. 163, 170 (Jan. 1993).

5. Hanley, *supra* note 3, at 13.

6. Ross Guberman, *Judges Speaking Softly: What They Long for When They Read*, Litigation, Summer 2018, at 48, 52.

crucial language."[7] Similarly, Judge Gerald Lebovits is of the view that quoting in general is a good thing but only if done "reasonably."[8] But he adds that quoting "excessively makes your document look choppy and you look lazy."[9]

Legal writing experts also agree that overquoting is more of a problem than underquoting. For example, Richard Neumann and Kristen Tiscione in their textbook inform students that the best and most persuasive descriptions of authorities are those provided in the writer's own words, and that block quotations are problematic and will "repel the reader."[10] They call a writer who uses too many quotations a "cut-and-paste artist," a derogatory term for legal writers.[11] Similarly, in *A Lawyer Writes*, the authors advise students to quote sparingly because there is no substitute for their own analysis.[12]

The top legal style guides give the same advice about minimizing quotations. For example, the *Redbook* is critical of lawyers who are nothing more than "quotation-gatherer[s]" because the result is dreary legal writing that no one wants to read.[13] Instead, legal writers should be reluctant to quote. Similarly, the *ALWD Guide* instructs writers to use quotations sparingly because when readers see too many quotations, they will be inclined to skip that material and/or conclude that the writer did not understand the material.[14]

While I agree with the above advice on overquoting, the problem is that novice legal writers will often state things inaccurately when putting things into their own words. Here is one example where, in paraphrasing, the standard for apparent authority was misstated—but first here is the correct standard:

---

7. *Id.*

8. Gerald Lebovits, *Do's, Don'ts, and Maybes: Legal Writing Do's—Part II*, N.Y. St. Bar Ass'n J., June 2007, at 64, 54.

9. *Id.*

10. Richard K. Neumann et al., Legal Reasoning and Legal Writing 224–25 (Wolters Kluwer 8th ed. 2017).

11. *Id.* at 226.

12. Christine Coughlin et al., A Lawyer Writes 111 (3d ed. 2018).

13. Redbook, *supra* note 2, at 155.

14. ALWD, *supra* note 2, at 392.

Apparent authority exists when a "principal has *intentionally or inadvertently* induced third persons to believe that such a person was its agent." *Canyon State Canners, Inc. v. Hooks*, 243 P.2d 1023, 1025 (Ariz. 1952).

Here is the incorrect paraphrase of this test, taken from a student's draft of an office memorandum:

Apparent authority exists when a principal has *reasonably* induced a third person to believe that such a person was its agent. *Canyon State Canners, Inc. v. Hooks*, 243 P.2d 1023, 1025 (Ariz. 1952).

In the paraphrase, the standard has been changed, and it is inaccurate because "intentionally or inadvertently" is not the same as "reasonably." The answer is not to always choose to quote the law or standard but to make sure that when you paraphrase, you have not inadvertently changed the meaning of the law.

B. Common Situations Where Quotations Are Appropriate

There are basically three common situations where you should quote: (1) the texts of statutes, rules, regulations, contracts, etc. that directly govern your case; (2) common-law legal tests courts have *explicitly* spelled out; and (3) "magical language" that courts use.[15] Let's take each of these situations in turn.

1. Statutes, Rules, Contracts, and the Like

When the wording of a statute controls the outcome of your case, you should quote the exact wording of the statute. In fact, if you were filing a brief in the United States Supreme Court, you would be required to do this under Rule 24(f), which provides that "constitutional provisions, treaties, statutes, ordinances, and regulations involved in the case [shall be] set out verbatim with appropriate citation."[16] When quoting statutory provisions, however, novice legal writers do not know how much of

---

15. *E.g.*, Hanley, *supra* note 3, at 13–14; *see also* Neumann et al., *supra* note 10, at 223.
16. Sup. Ct. R. 24(f).

the statute to quote because many statutory provisions are very long and include many more provisions and words than are needed to resolve the dispute at hand. As a result, students tend to overquote.

Let's look at an example. Assume you have been asked to determine in an office memorandum whether people can burglarize their own home (the hypothetical I used with my first-year students involved a separated couple, so the husband still co-owned the home and had a key but had temporarily moved out and was living with a friend). Arizona law applies, and two statutes, one defining burglary, and one defining "enter or remain unlawfully," are relevant:

In Arizona, second-degree burglary is defined as follows:

> **A.** A person commits burglary in the second degree by entering or remaining unlawfully in or on a residential structure with the intent to commit any theft or any felony therein.
> **B.** Burglary in the second degree is a class 3 felony.[17]

"Enter or remain unlawfully" is defined as:

> an act of a person who enters or remains on premises when the person's intent for so entering or remaining is not licensed, authorized or otherwise privileged except when the entry is to commit theft of merchandise displayed for sale during normal business hours, when the premises are open to the public and when the person does not enter any unauthorized areas of the premises.[18]

On their first drafts, many students quoted both statutes in their entirety, which is unnecessary because not all parts of these statutes are relevant to the issue. Here is one way to take these two statutes and boil them down to their essence while still quoting the essential words:

> In Arizona, "[a] person commits burglary in the second degree by entering or remaining unlawfully in or on a residential structure with the intent to commit any theft or any felony therein." A.R.S. § 13-1507(A). Unlawful entry is further defined

---

17. Ariz. Rev. Stat. Ann. § 13-1507.
18. *Id.* § 13-1501(2).

as entering or remaining on the premises when the person's intent is not "licensed, authorized or otherwise privileged." A.R.S. § 13-1501(2).

Therefore, when you quote statutory provisions, quote only as much of those provisions as are needed to resolve the issue. The same is true of a specific rule or regulation that may control the outcome of a case.

Another place you need to quote is if something in writing controls the outcome of a case, such as a contract, a deed, a will, a provision of an insurance policy, or a similar writing. Obviously, if you are asking the court to interpret any of these things, the court is going to need to read the exact wording at issue.

2. Common Law Legal Tests

Cases are not only governed by statutes or rules; courts also decide cases based on legal tests courts have articulated through the common law. For example, let's say you are asked to determine whether an eyewitness's pretrial identification of a defendant was "reliable." The United States Supreme Court has devised a test for making that determination, and many states have adopted it:

> [T]he factors to be considered [in evaluating the likelihood of misidentification] include the opportunity of the witness to view the criminal at the time of the crime, the witness' degree of attention, the accuracy of his prior description of the criminal, the level of certainty demonstrated at the confrontation, and the time between the crime and the confrontation.[19]

You would want to quote this test or at least the key parts of it because it is recognized as the established test for reliability, with virtually the same impact as if it were part of a statute.

3. Magical Language

You also want to quote when the passage or the words you want to use are perfectly suited to your situation; in other words, they are magical.

---

19. State v. Lehr, 38 P.3d 1172, 1184 (Ariz. 2002) (*quoting* Manson v. Braithwaite, 432 U.S. 98, 114 (1977)).

As stated in *Legal Reasoning and Legal Writing,* quoting works when the words "*with remarkable economy,*" put the reader in touch with the thinking of a court, legislature, or expert in the field; or... are *the most eloquent and succinct conceivable* expression of an important idea."[20] In other words, you could not improve upon the message by paraphrasing. But even when you find that magical language, as with statutory wording, you only want to quote the critical words and put everything else in your own words.

Let's continue with our example of a pre-trial identification of a defendant by an eyewitness. Assume that the witness testified that her attention was "riveted" on the assailant (in a hypothetical designed on this subject, the witness, who only viewed the assailant for 10 seconds, had been an Olympic archery expert as well). Assume there are cases where courts have found that the pretrial identification was reliable, in part, because the witness's attention was "riveted" upon the attacker. You would consider quoting that passage, including the word "riveted," because it is the exact same word your witness used:

> Even if there is a short window of time, the witness's degree of attention can support a finding of reliability if circumstances drew the witness's attention to the suspect. *State v. Alvarez,* 701 P.2d 1178, 1180 (Ariz. 1985). In *Alvarez,* the Court held that even though the witness was only able to observe the suspect for three seconds, she was particularly attentive because she was afraid of being killed. *Id.* The Court reasoned, "[W]here a victim rivets her attention upon her attacker, the reliability of her subsequent identification... is enhanced." *Id. See also State v. McLoughlin,* 652 P.2d 531, 535 (Ariz. 1982) (witnesses in parking lot were "riveted" on an assailant rushing out of a store with a gun in hand).

Therefore, the word "riveted" is magical because the witness in your case and in a reported case used similar wording, and this wording, in part, led the court to find that the pretrial identification was reliable.

---

20. NEUMANN ET AL., *supra* note 10, at 222–23.

.

4. Other Situations Where Quoting Is Appropriate

While the above three situations are the most common situations when quoting is appropriate, there are a few others. If your situation involves the testimony of witnesses, there are times you will quote that testimony verbatim. Further, if you use a term of art (a legal term) from a statute or case, you will want to quote it the first time from its source, such as a statute, but after that first reference, you can use the word or words without quotations as part of your analysis or argument.[21] For example, let's say you are dealing with whether an intoxicated defendant had "actual physical control" of a vehicle, a term contained in statutes all over the country. The first time you reference actual physical control, you put it in quotes, but after that, you can leave the quotes off.

You should also use quotation marks around words used to mean "so-called-but-not-really."[22] Using quotation marks around the word or words themselves will signal the "so-called" meaning without using the term directly. Here is an example with the inclusion of the "so-called" wording, which you would want to omit:

> My so-called "best friend" testified against me at my trial.

Another example where you would use quotation marks is when you are being ironic. The use of quotation marks will inform your reader that you are saying something in jest.[23] This is like adding a wink to your sentence. Do not, however, use them for sarcasm or ridicule because your audience may find this usage disrespectful. Here is an example: The plaintiff's "injuries" consist of nothing more than a cut on the elbow.

C. Rules Applying to Quotations

Now that you have a better idea of when to quote and when not to, let's turn to some guidelines for quoting once you decide that you should quote. This list will cover the primary issues you will face when quoting in legal writing.

---

21. Redbook, *supra* note 2, at 25.
22. *Id.* at 29.
23. *Id.* at 30.

1. Accuracy

Your quotations need to be 100% accurate. If you have not quoted accurately, this will negatively impact your credibility with your audience.[24] That means if you make *any* alterations, even minor ones, such as changing the capitalization of a letter to fit within the syntax of a sentence or adding italics because you want to emphasize a word or words, you need to indicate those changes to your reader. We will address how you show changes and alterations later in this section.

2. Block Quotations and Lead-Ins

Special rules govern the use of block quotations. First, you only use them if a quotation is 50 or more words.[25] Second, when you use them, you single-space the quoted language, and you separate the block quotation from the text above and below it with a blank line, creating a surrounding form of white space.[26] Third, you do not put quotation marks around the block indent, and you put the citation supporting the block quotation on the next line at the left margin.[27] Fourth, you only indent the first line of a paragraph if that word is also the first word of a paragraph in the source being quoted.[28] Here is an example of a block quotation with a lead-in from a brief filed in the United States Supreme Court:

> The Court of Appeals was incorrect because retroactivity is about remedies, not rights. The retroactivity of criminal procedure rules determines the scope of the exclusionary rule when law changes:
>
> > [T]he source of a "new rule" is the Constitution itself, not any judicial power to create new rules of law. Accordingly, the

---

24. *E.g.*, Teresa J. Reid Rambo & Leanne J. Pflaum, Legal Writing by Design 519 (2d ed. 2013); Neumann, et al., *supra* note 10, at 226 (noting that supervisors, judges, and teachers can easily spot inaccuracies in quotations and lose some confidence in you because you have not been careful).

25. The Bluebook: A Uniform System of Citation R. 5.1(a), at 397 (Columbia L. Rev. Ass'n et al. eds, 21st ed. 2020) [hereinafter Bluebook].

26. ALWD, *supra* note 2, at 397.

27. If you are writing a law review article, however, and you want to include a footnote after the block indent, you place the footnote at the end of the block indent itself. ALWD, *supra* note 14, at 400.

28. Bluebook, *supra* note 25, at 83.

underlying right necessarily pre-exists our articulation of the new rule. What we are actually determining when we assess the "retroactivity" of a new rule is not the temporal scope of a newly announced right, but whether a violation of the right that occurred prior to the announcement of the new rule will entitle a criminal defendant to the relief sought.[29]

Danforth v. Minnesota, 552 U.S. 264, 271 (2008).

Notice the lead-in sentence in the above example. Instead of a free-standing block quotation, the writer introduced the block quotation with a substantive, persuasive, and succinct introduction that focused the reader on why the block quotation was important.[30] And because many judges skip block quotations altogether, that introduction to the block quotation can itself communicate the key argument without even reading the quotation. For that reason, you should avoid using the lazy lead-ins that most lawyers use (yes, I too am guilty), which do not serve to inform your reader about the purpose of the quotation. Lazy lead-ins include: "The court stated," "The statute reads, in pertinent part, as follows," and, "The witness testified as follows."[31] Those types of lead-ins are "the death knell to a good quotation."[32] Finally, put the point of the quotation into your own words (as opposed to just repeating information already contained in the block quotation).

3. Punctuation with Quotation Marks

Students often make mistakes when it comes to placement of punctuation marks with quotation marks. There are a few simple rules to remember:

---

29. Brief for the Petitioner at 31, Davis v. United States, 564 U.S. 229 (2011) (No. 09-11328), 2010 WL 5168874, at *17.

30. *See, e.g.*, Guberman, *supra* note 6, at 52; Hanley, *supra* note 3, at (warning not to paste quoted text into your writing and then "expect the reader to discern the original author's idea or its relevance to your argument. Instead, write an introduction to the quotation that summarizes the quotation's meaning or explains its importance."); *Legal Writing Tip: Introduce Block Quotes*, Bar Ass'n of S.F. (June 12, 2018), https://www.sfbar.org/blog/legal-writing-tip-introduce-block-quotes/ ("the lead-in is your assertion. The quote is its support.").

31. Redbook, *supra* note 2, at 164.

32. *Id.*

1. Use a comma to introduce a direct quotation of fewer than 50 words (Ex: He said, "I saw that woman run the red light.").[33]

2. You can use a colon instead, but only if you use a more formal device to introduce the quotation and the introduction is an independent clause (Ex: The alien had this to say when it landed on Earth: "Protect the environment because we do not have enough room for you on our planet.").

3. Do not use a comma or a colon if the quotation is folded into the syntax of the sentence (Ex: The judge told the attorneys that they must "arrive to the courthouse on time or be sanctioned.").[34]

4. *Periods and commas go inside quotation marks.* If you are wondering why I italicized that sentence, it is because this is a rule students violate often: they put the period or comma *outside* the quotation marks. It is not just students that make this mistake. One appellate judge in Illinois, Judge Painter, listed the placement of periods and commas outside quotation marks as one of the most common mistakes he has seen in legal writing, estimating that lawyers are incorrect "30% of the time."[35] In fact, it appears as if all writers, not just legal writers, make this mistake (at least in the United States; in England, it is proper to place periods and commas outside quotation marks), because in *Dreyer's English*, a guide for all writers, the author has this to say about commas and periods with quotation marks: "Though semicolons, because they are elusive and enigmatic and they like it that way, are set outside terminal quotation marks, periods and commas—and if I make this point once, I'll make it a thousand times, and trust me, I will—are always set inside. Always."[36]

5. Final semicolons and colons go outside the quotation marks.

6. Example: The court found that the shelter was a "place of overnight repose and safety"; accordingly, it concluded that the provisions of the Fair Housing Act applied.

---

33. *Id.* at 9.

34. *Id.* at 10.

35. *Judge Painter: The Most Common Errors I See*, LEGAL WRITING PRO, https://www.legalwritingpro.com/articles/judge-painter-common-errors-see/ (last visited Jan. 29, 2022).

36. DREYER, *supra* note 1, at 55.

7. Question marks and exclamation marks may go inside or outside, depending on their location in the original quotation (follow where it is in the original quotation). For example, the Supreme Court asked this question: "Why do Louisiana and Oregon allow nonunanimous convictions?"[37] Because the question mark is part of the quoted material, it goes before the quotes. However, if the question mark is not part of the original quotation, it belongs outside, as in this example: In assessing whether an employee created a software program for an employer or not, courts have asked, is the work "included as part of the employee's job description"?

That is all you need to remember about punctuation and quotation marks.

4. Ellipses, Brackets, and Italics

Our next topic is how to use ellipses, brackets, and italics when you alter quotations. **Warning**: These rules can be somewhat tedious, so do not operate heavy machinery while reading this section. Your other option is to take a nap before reading this or grab a cup of coffee. Just keep in mind that lawyers, or at least many of us, love this stuff.

An ellipsis, which is not to be confused with an eclipse, consists of three dots or periods indicating an omission of words. These three little dots or periods tend to confuse students, so here are some rules about them. First, *never, never, never* begin a sentence with an ellipsis, whether that sentence is an entire sentence or just a quoted phrase.[38] Second, do not use an ellipsis when only an individual word is altered; use brackets instead.[39] Third, do not indicate omission of matters before or after a quotation where the quoted language is worked into the flow of the sentence or where the quotation ends at a period or other final punctuation, but *do* indicate omission of matter *within* a phrase or clause with an ellipsis.[40] This rule is a bit tricky, so let me give you an example. Here is the full quotation:

---

37. Ramos v. Louisiana, 140 S.Ct. 1390, 1394 (2020).
38. *See* ALWD, *supra* note 2, at 410–11; BLUEBOOK, *supra* note 25, at 86.
39. *See* BLUEBOOK, *supra* note 25, at 86.
40. *Id.*

In its capacity as a public employer, the state bears special constitutional burdens. Notably, the First Amendment restricts the state's ability to fire employees who speak out on matters of public concern. But this doctrine is limited; after all, the First Amendment does not require a public office to be run as a roundtable for employee complaints over internal office affairs.[41]

Let's say you only want to use a portion of the second sentence and fold it into the syntax of the sentence like this:

> The Ninth Circuit has stressed that "the First Amendment restricts the state's ability to fire employees who speak out on matters of public concern."

There is no need to include an ellipsis either at the beginning or at the end of the quotation.

Let's say you only want to quote part of a sentence and omit the middle part, like this:

> While public employees have some protections, "this doctrine is limited; after all, the First Amendment does not require a public office to be run as a roundtable… over internal office affairs."

You *do* need to include an ellipsis because you have omitted the middle of a sentence.

Let's say you only want to quote the *entire* middle sentence like this:

> The Ninth Circuit has emphasized restrictions on the state as follows: "Notably, the First Amendment restricts the state's ability to fire employees who speak out on matters of public concern."

There is no need for an ellipsis either at the beginning or at the end of the sentence because you are quoting the entire sentence.

Another point about using ellipses is that if you use quoted language as a standalone sentence and you omit the end of the quoted sentence, you need to add a period—so you will have four dots.[42] Here is an example:

---

41. Weeks v. Bayer, 246 F.3d 1231, 1233 (9th Cir. 2001) (internal quotation marks and citation omitted).

42. BLUEBOOK, *supra* note 25, at 86–87.

"The First Amendment restricts the state's ability to fire employees...."

The final tricky thing about ellipses is how to space them. They should be three spaced periods with spaces in between them.[43] In other words, it looks like this: "Where... Congress has acted, the states should not legislate in that area." It should not look like this: "Where ... Congress has acted, the states should not legislate in that area." Got that?

Now, let's move on to the use of brackets. There are essentially three situations where you will use brackets.[44] First, if you alter how a letter is capitalized, you need brackets. For example, if the letter "A" in the original passage was capitalized, but you want to change that to a small "a" to fit within the syntax of the sentence, you do this: "[a]." The second situation occurs when you alter or omit one or more letters in a word. For example, if you want to change the verb from "state" in the original to "stating" in the altered version, you will denote that by doing this: "stat[ing]." Further, when you omit letters entirely, such as turning the word "employees" into "employee," you denote that by using empty brackets: "employee[]." The final situation is when you substitute or add words to a quotation, as in this example:

> Original passage: The court sanctioned Mr. James Ogilvie for including too many typographical and grammatical errors in his brief.
>
> Altered passage: The court sanctioned [the lawyer] for including too many typographical and grammatical errors in his brief.

As with overquoting, beware of overusing brackets. While legal writers tend to be proud of using brackets to show off their knowledge of the technicalities of using them, too many can interfere in the flow of a sentence.[45] Instead, you should consider paraphrasing.

---

43. *See* REDBOOK, *supra* note 2, at 41.

44. *See* ALWD, *supra* note 2, at 403.

45. Bryan A. Garner, *Parenthetical Habits: On the Use and Overuse of Parentheses and Brackets* (Nov. 1, 2016, 2:10 AM), https://www.abajournal.com/magazine/article/garner_parenthetical_habits.

The final change you may make is emphasizing words in the passage that were not emphasized in the original. You do this by using italics, but you need to show your reader you made this change by adding (emphasis added).[46]

Here is an example of the original quotation without the emphasis added:

> The Ninth Circuit has made clear that when a public employee speaks out about misuse of public funds, it is a matter of public concern protected by the First Amendment:
>> "[W]e have stated that misuse of public funds, wastefulness, and inefficiency in managing and operating government entities are matters of inherent public concern."[47] *Johnson*, 48 F.3d at 425.

Here is that same quotation with the emphasis added by the writer:

> The Ninth Circuit has made clear that when a public employee speaks out about misuse of public funds, it is a matter of public concern protected by the First Amendment:
>> "[W]e have stated that *misuse of public funds*, wastefulness, and inefficiency in managing and operating government entities are matters of inherent public concern."[48] *Johnson*, 48 F.3d at 425 (emphasis added).

5. Sic

Students love to use *sic*, and I must admit that as a law student, I loved it as well: because I knew so little, it boosted my confidence to catch a court's spelling, typographical, or grammatical error. In general, be judicious when using *sic* to correct such errors. Use it only when accuracy is critical, such as when you are quoting a statute, rule, or legal test.[49] Certain very minor errors can be silently corrected without indicating

---

46. ALWD, *supra* note 2, at 404; Bluebook, *supra* note 25, at 84–85.
47. Johnson v. Multnomah Cnty., 48 F.3d 420, 425 (9th Cir. 1995).
48. *Id.*
49. Redbook, *supra* note 2, at 36.

the change,[50] and if your goal is to embarrass your opponent by pointing out a mistake in your opponent's writing, resist the temptation.[51] Instead, you can correct the error yourself and use brackets to show an alteration. If you do use *sic*, here is how:

> "The court hold [*sic*] that the plaintiff's complaint should be dismissed."

Although I have suggested minimizing the use of *sic*, I do not want to leave you with the impression that if you make a lot of mistakes in your writing that you submit to a court, it will not notice. It will. For example, in *Sanches v. Carrollton–Farmers Branch Independent School District*,[52] the plaintiff's lawyers wrote this in their opening brief, and the court, in quoting it, was not shy about pointing out the errors using *sic* throughout:

> The Magistrate's egregious errors in its [*sic*][53] failure to utilize or apply the law constitute extraordinary circumstances, justifying vacateur [*sic*] of the assignment to [*sic*] Magistrate…. Because a magistrate is not an Article III judge, his incompetence in applying general principals [*sic*] of law are [*sic*] extraordinary.[54]

The court criticized the writing, explaining that the "sentences are so poorly written that it is difficult to decipher what the attorneys mean… and the quoted passage is an unjustified and most unprofessional and disrespectful attack."[55] The court also noted what while it did not normally comment on technical and grammatical errors because occasional mistakes are made by everyone, "here the miscues are so egregious and obvious and an average fourth grader would have avoided most

---

50. *Id.* at 158–59 (listing examples, such as changing double quotation marks to single quotation marks or vice versa, punctuation relative to quotation marks, or curly quotes instead of straight ones).

51. *Id.* at 36.

52. 647 F.3d 156 (5th Cir. 2011).

53. Note that even though the Fifth Circuit italicized the word "sic," both Bluebook and ALWD provide that the word is not italicized. *See* Bluebook, *supra* note 25, at 84; ALWD, *supra* note 14, at 406.

54. *Sanches*, 647 F.3d at 172.

55. *Id.*

of them."[56] The court wrapped up by saying that it was ironic that the lawyers used the word "incompetence" because "the only thing that is incompetent is the passage itself."[57] Therefore, while you do not want to go crazy correcting your opponent's errors, if your opponent makes lots of mistakes (or if you do), be prepared for someone—maybe even a court—to comment on it.

6. Quotations Within Quotations

To punctuate a quotation within a short quotation (as opposed to a block indent quotation), use double quotations around the entire quotation and single quotes around the internal quotation.[58] If you are using a block quotation, and there is a quotation within a quotation, use double quotes around the internal quotation.[59]

7. Types of Quotation Marks

This is where it gets fun because there are many kinds of quotation marks, and they have been given various nicknames. Who knew that there were more species of quotation marks than there are birds? Some kinds have been called neutral, vertical, straight, typewriter, or dumb quotes.[60] Others have been called typographic or curly quotes. Yet others have been called smart quotes and ambidextrous quotes.[61]

Let's define a few key terms before getting into the mysteries surrounding these different quotation marks. Neutral or "dumb" quotation marks are straight quotes that look like this: " I am not sure why you would insult these marks by calling them dumb; they look sharp to me.

The other kind of quotation mark is the "smart" quotation mark, also known as "curly" quotation marks. They look like this: " " The *Chicago*

---

56. *Id.* at 172 n.13.

57. *Id.*

58. ALWD, *supra* note 2, at 395; *see also* BLUEBOOK, *supra* note 25, at 85.

59. ALWD, *supra* note 2, at 397; *see also* BLUEBOOK, *supra* note 25, at 86.

60. *Quotation Marks in English*, WIKIPEDIA, https://en.wikipedia.org/wiki/Quotation_marks_in_English (last visited Jan. 29, 2022).

61. *"and ' straight or curly?*, LEGAL WRITING PROF BLOG (Aug. 20, 2008), https://lawprofessors.typepad.com/legalwriting/2008/08/and-straight-or.html.

Manual of Style provides that published works should use "smart" quotes (like the ones I just used).[62]

Computers used to use the ugly and dumb straight marks,[63] and I know my word program defaults to the curly, smart quotes. Apparently, however, they still show up randomly (for example, if you cut and paste from internet sources that use dumb straight quotes) and, according to the *Redbook*, give a document an "amateurish look."[64] (Personally, I am starting to feel sorry for the straight quotes because they cannot help what they look like.)

Interestingly, although the *Redbook* counsels against using them, in the Legal Writing Prof Blog, a reader asked whether the legal writing community prefers straight (also called ambidextrous) or curly quotes, and the response was that there was "no consensus on the format of quotation marks... in the legal writing community" but to be consistent.[65]

There are a couple of small complications involving the use of curly quotes. If your computer defaults to using them (as mine does), it can create issues when you want to talk about feet and inches using marks, and when you use apostrophes. Single and double-quotation marks do not work when you are trying to express something in inches and feet.[66] It's not, she is 5' 6" tall. It is, she is 5′ 6″ tall. If you look closely, you will see the difference. To make the notations for inches and feet, you press Alt+8242 for prime (the single mark) and Alt+8243 for double prime (the inches mark).[67] Another time you might end up using an incorrect mark is for apostrophes. The danger arises when you use an opening closing mark instead of a closing mark in a contraction like this: "He was born in '94." That is incorrect. It should be, "He was born in '94." You can make sure you get the right mark by either typing both single quotes and

---

62. *"Smart" Quotation Marks*, CHI. MANUAL OF STYLE ONLINE ch. 6.115, https://www.chicagomanualofstyle.org/book/ed17/part2/ch06/psec115.html (last visited Jan. 29, 2022).

63. REDBOOK, *supra* note 2, at 25.

64. *Id.*

65. LEGAL WRITING PROF BLOG, *supra* note 61.

66. REDBOOK, *supra* note 2, at 25.

67. *Word: Insert Prime and Double Prime Characters*, CYBERTEXT CONSULTING: CYBERTEXT NEWSLETTER (Sept. 23, 2018), https://cybertext.wordpress.com/2018/09/23/word-insert-a-prime-and-double-prime-characters/.

then deleting the wrong one or by inputting a single straight quote using your keypad as described above.

D. Cleaned-Up Quotations

The final topic we will address is the use of cleaned-up quotations. The use of cleaned-up quotations is an emerging trend in quoting in legal writing, and my prediction is that it will soon be the preferred way to quote passages. Let me tell you what a cleaned-up quotation is, when and why cleaned-up quotations first began as a movement, and how cleaned-up quotations are currently being used.

What are they? If a quotation has the words "cleaned up" in parentheses following a quotation, that means that the author has: (1) removed extraneous non-substantive material like brackets, quotation marks, and internal citations; (2) changed capitalization without using brackets to indicate the change; and (3) in doing so, has represented that the alterations were made solely to enhance readability and otherwise faithfully reproduces the quoted text.[68] One thing is clear: You cannot and must not make any change in the substance of the quotation.[69]

Here is an example of the original statement:

> "Without a showing of direct responsibility for the improper action, liability will not lie against a supervisory official. A causal connection, or an affirmative link, between the misconduct complained of and the official sued is necessary." *Wolf-Lillie,* 699 F.2d at 869.[70]

Here is how a court subsequently quoted this language using a cleaned-up quotation:

> "Without a showing of direct responsibility for the improper action, liability will not lie against a supervisory official. A causal connection, or an affirmative link, between the misconduct

---

68. Jack Metzler, *Cleaning up Quotations,* 18 J. App. Prac. & Process 143 (2017).
69. Redbook, *supra* note 2, at 159.
70. Rascon v. Hardiman, 803 F.2d 269, 273 (7th Cir. 1986).

complained of and the official sued is necessary." *Id.* (cleaned up).[71]

Note that the only alteration in the second quotation is the omission of a "quoting" parenthetical with a citation to the *Wolf-Lillie* case. If the court hadn't used "cleaned up," the full citation would have read: "*Id.* (quoting *Wolf-Lillie v. Sonquist*, 699 F.2d 864, 869 (7th Cir. 1983))." But everything else is the same.

The primary reason for this method is that because judges and lawyers commonly use quotations in their writing, a quotation may contain internal references,[72] internal quoting, and so many nested quotations within nested quotations, the reader may feel like a prisoner in a hornet's nest. The need to be perfectly accurate conflicts with a reader's need to understand the context without distractions. In other words, 100% accuracy impedes readability. And while style guides provide rules for how to cite every layer of quotation, the problem is the "extra baggage" that often produces.[73] The result is that needless time and energy are consumed wading through these quotations.

In 2017, author Jack Metzler wrote an article advocating "cleaned-up" quotations,[74] and now they are becoming more and more common. While the *Bluebook* rejected Metzler's suggestion of adding a rule to allow for them,[75] the *ALWD Guide* acknowledged that a few scholars have advocated for their use but recommended avoiding them unless you know that your supervisor or the court approves.[76] The *Redbook* goes even further and suggests that writers should "consider" a "cleaned-up" quotation to avoid "ostentatious pedantry" when quoting quotations within quotations.[77]

---

71. Gomez v. Rihani, No. 1:19-CV-08437, 2021 WL 1165095, at *3 (N.D. Ill. Mar. 26, 2021).

72. Metzler, *supra* note 69, at 143−44, 151.

73. *Id.* at 146.

74. Metzler, *supra* note 69; *see also* Redbook, *supra* note 2, at 160 (giving Metzler credit for being the "signal innovator").

75. *Compare* Metzler, *supra* note 69, at 154 (proposing a new Rule 5.4 for cleaned-up quotations) *with* Bluebook, *supra* note 25, at X, 87 (not containing a Rule 5.4).

76. ALWD, *supra* note 2, at 406.

77. Redbook, *supra* note 2, at 159. *But see* Tessa L. Dysart, *Clean Up Your House, Your Car, Your Life—Not your Citations*, L. Professor Blogs Network: App. Advoc.

In a twist of irony, the courts appear to be taking the lead in using them, even though the *Bluebook* did not take Metzler up on his advice to add a rule allowing for them. All circuits and the U.S. Supreme Court have used them.[78] Further, while some courts take the time to explain their usage,[79] other courts simply use them without explanation.

Cleaned-up quotations are appropriate if your audience—whether that is a legal writing professor, a supervisor, or a court—agrees. As a legal writing professor, I instruct students not to use cleaned-up quotations, so they know how to use internal quotations and cites because it is easier to learn how to eliminate some non-substantive part of quotations after first learning how to include these parts of the quotation.

In conclusion, now you know more than you ever wanted to know about why to quote only in specific situations and, when you do, where the punctuation belongs. You have also learned about how to use cleaned-up quotations, assuming your audience approves. And finally, you can impress your friends because you will be the only one that knows the nicknames that exist for quotation marks.

BLOG (Oct. 18, 2021), https://lawprofessors.typepad.com/appellate_advocacy/2021/10/clean-up-your-house-your-car-your-life-not-your-citations.html (opining that it is one thing for judges to use them, but lawyers should not because they already have issues with misstating the law and the record and so a brief full of cleaned-up citations would cause a judge to carefully check each cite).

78. United States v. Rodriguez-Monserrate, 22 F.4th 35, 42 (1st Cir. 2021); Yukos Cap. S.A.R.L. v. Feldman, 977 F.3d 216, 233 (2d Cir. 2020); United States v. Johnson, 19 F.4th 248, 256 (3rd Cir. 2021); United States v. Lozano, 962 F.3d 773, 778 (4th Cir. 2020); Future Proof Brands, L.L.C. v. Molson Coors Beverage Co., 982 F.3d 280, 288 (5th Cir. 2020); Glennborough Homeowners Ass'n v. U.S. Postal Serv., 21 F.4th 410, 414 (6th Cir. 2021); Driftless Area Land Conservancy v. Valcq, 16 F.4th 508, 521 (7th Cir. 2021); United States v. Oliver, 987 F.3d 794, 799 (8th Cir. 2021); Cal. Trucking Ass'n v. Bonta, 996 F.3d 644, 653 (9th Cir. 2021); Wimberly v. Williams, 14 F.4th 1140, 1144 (10th Cir. 2021); United States v. Fleury, 20 F.4th 1353, 1364 (11th Cir. 2021); United States v. Tucker, 12 F.4th 804, 813 (D.C. Cir. 2021); Intel Corp. v. Qualcomm Inc., 21 F.4th 784, 790 (Fed. Cir. 2021); Brownback v. King, 141 S. Ct. 740, 748 (2021).

79. *E.g.*, Gomez v. Rihani, No. 1:19-CV-08437, 2021 WL 1165095, at *2 n.5 (N.D. Ill. Mar. 26, 2021) (noting that the "opinion uses (cleaned up) to indicate that internal quotation marks, alterations, and citations have been omitted from quotations.").

10

Zebra Crossings, Railroad Tracks, and Parallel Bars

Why You Should Use Parallel Construction in Your Writing

....

In searching for a metaphor to describe parallelism, I did an internet search for things in life that are parallel. The term "zebra crossings" kept coming up, and I was surprised to learn that there are crossings made just for zebras. Where in the world is there such a critical mass of zebras that special crossings are required? Can zebras see the colors of the traffic lights? Are giraffes allowed to use them too?

After extricating myself from the rabbit hole of zebra crossings,[1] I refocused on legal writing. Why is parallelism relevant to legal writing? The same reason it is important for parallel bars, railroad tracks, and zebra crossings: It keeps things moving efficiently in the right direction and prevents bad things from happening. If a gymnast gets on bars that are slightly off, or a train travels down railroad tracks that are out of line, you can expect a bad result. And while I am not certain that crooked lines in a zebra crossing would cause damage, I do know that using parallelism in your legal writing can move your audience along and keep them on track.

---

1. In case you do not know what a zebra crossing is, it can be found in England, and it is a crosswalk that has broad white stripes where vehicles must stop if pedestrians wish to cross. The stripes, which are parallel, resemble the pattern on a zebra. Kat Eschner, *A Short History of the Crosswalk*, SMITHSONIAN MAG. (Oct. 31, 2017), https://www.smithsonianmag.com/smart-news/short-history-crosswalk-180965339/. And you thought you would not learn anything new by reading this chapter.

A. What Is Parallelism?

Parallelism or parallel construction "requires that expressions similar in content and function be outwardly similar. The likeness of form enables the reader to recognize more readily the likeness of content and function."[2] To create parallelism, "place a pair or series of words, phrases, clauses, or sentences in similar grammatical structure."[3]

When it comes to parallelism, definitions help, but it is easier to see how it works with examples.

Here is an example of non-parallel construction from a former student writing about the facts of a hypothetical I gave the class:

> The defendant had co-ownership of the home, he does not intend to leave it, and he also had a key to it.

Note that this is a list of facts that support the defendant's ownership of his home, but this list is not parallel, disrupting the flow of the sentence. Here are those same ideas but using a parallel construction:

> He **co-owned** the home, he **intended** to stay, and he **retained** a key.

Notice that "co-owned," "intended" and "retained" are all past-tense verbs, so they all match. It is easier to follow the meaning of the sentence if this parallel construction is used.

Why is parallel construction important in legal writing? It can help with eloquence, balance, and rhythm.[4] (Notice that this list is parallel: I did not say it can make our writing eloquent, create balance, and it also helps with rhythm.) Beyond those goals, parallelism can add clarity because it is a way to "streamline information and make your points stick."[5] And on top of that, it is a rhetorical technique that can help persuade

---

2. William Strunk, Jr. & E. B. White, The Elements of Style 26 (4th ed., Longman 1999).

3. Teresa J. Reid Rambo & Leanne J. Pflaum, Legal Writing by Design 516 (2d ed. 2013).

4. *See, e.g., id.* at 243; Susie Salmon, *Keep it Parallel*, Ariz. Att'y, Sept. 2014, at 10, 10.

5. Ross Guberman, *Five Ways to Write Like John Roberts*, Legal Writing Pro (Mar. 2010) [hereinafter *Write Like John Roberts*], https://www.legalwritingpro.com/pdf/john-roberts.pdf.

your reader.[6] In fact, legal writing expert Ross Guberman has identified the use of parallelism as a critical skill worth mastering because it is "highly correlated with broader measures of writing ability."[7] Given all the goals that the use of parallel construction can accomplish, what's not to love?

B. Examples of Parallelism

Before we get into the mechanics of how to write using parallel construction, let us look at some examples of parallelism outside of the legal writing world to help prove that the device works not only in legal writing but in other areas our lives including music and speeches.

Let's start with music; when I think of words like balance and rhythm, I think about my favorite songs. While we might not remember what our property professor had to say about the rule against perpetuities, we do have an incredible knack for remembering every word of our favorite songs—especially the chorus. Maybe it is because in many songs, the writer uses parallel construction.

Let's take Pharrell Williams and his song, "Happy." Here is the chorus, and notice how he uses parallel construction:

> Huh (Because I'm happy)
> Clap along if you feel like a room without a roof
>   (Because I'm happy)
> Clap along if you feel like happiness is the truth
>   (Because I'm happy)
> Clap along if you know what happiness is to you
>   (Because I'm happy)
> Clap along if you feel like that's what you wanna do[8]

---

6. *See* Rachel H. Smith, *The Unparalleled Benefits of Teaching Parallelism*, Second Draft, Spring 2019, at 26, 28.

7. Ross Guberman, *Six Rules You Should Master—And I Can Prove it!* Legal Writing Pro (Feb. 24, 2015), https://www.legalwritingpro.com/blog/six-rules-you-should-master-and-i-can-prove-it/.

8. Pharrell Williams, *Happy, on* Despicable Me 2: Original Motion Picture Soundtrack (Back Lot Music 2013), at 00:24–00:48.

After each "clap along," the structure is parallel. There is balance and rhythm, and if he had not used this construction, the song might have been a dud instead of the blockbuster it was.

Another example is the song, "Ain't No Mountain High Enough" recorded by Marvin Gaye and Tammi Terrell (and later used in *Remember the Titans*, one of my favorite movies). Here is that song's chorus:

> Cause baby, there ain't no mountain high enough
> Ain't no valley low enough,
> Ain't no river wide enough
> To keep me from getting to you, baby[9]

Notice that the words, "mountain high enough," "valley low enough," and "river wide enough," are all parallel to create both balance and rhythm.

Now, let's look at some famous speeches. John F. Kennedy said this in his inaugural address:

> Let every nation know, whether it wishes us well or ill, that we shall pay any price, bear any burden, meet any hardship, support any friend, oppose any foe to assure the survival and the success of liberty.[10]

Did you spot the parallelism? The phrases, "pay any price," "bear any burden," "meet any hardship," "support any friend," and "oppose any foe" are all parallel. Even "the survival," and "the success" are parallel in that both use the article "the" before the noun.

Here is another example, this time from a speech that President George W. Bush gave on terrorism on Sept. 20, 2001:

> We have seen the state of our union in the endurance of rescuers, working past exhaustion. We've seen the unfurling of flags,

---

9. MARVIN GAYE & TAMMI TERRELL, *Ain't No Mountain High Enough, on* REMEMBER THE TITANS: AN ORIGINAL WALT DISNEY MOTION PICTURE SOUNDTRACK (Walt Disney Records 2000), at 00:29–00:44.

10. John F. Kennedy, Inaugural Address (Jan. 20, 1961), in THE INAUGURAL ADDRESSES OF THE PRESIDENTS 427, 428 (John Gabriel Hunt, ed., 1997).

the lighting of candles, the giving of blood, the saying of prayers—in English, Hebrew, and Arabic.[11]

The words "unfurling," "lighting," "giving," and "saying" are parallel. There is a smooth flow to the words, making them clear and easy to follow.

C. Parallelism in Legal Writing

Let's now focus our attention on parallelism in legal writing specifically. You might think that a court, especially the United States Supreme Court, would not concern itself with an unimportant matter of style like parallelism. You would be wrong. In Lockhart v. United States,[12] the issue involved the interpretation of a statute setting forth when a defendant is subject to an increased maximum sentence if convicted of possessing child pornography.[13] The statute in question provided that a defendant convicted of child pornography would be subject to a 10-year mandatory minimum sentence and an increased maximum sentence if they have "a prior conviction... under the laws of any State relating to aggravated sexual abuse, sexual abuse, or abusive sexual conduct involving a minor or ward."[14] The specific issue was whether the terms "involving a ward or minor" only modified the words "abusive sexual conduct" or modified the other parts of the list contained in the statute.

That issue sparked a whole discussion about the use of nouns or verbs in a series where there is a straightforward parallel construction, a point causing disagreement among the Justices. A leading treatise on statutory construction provided that "When there is a straightforward, parallel construction that involves all nouns or verbs in a series," a modifier at the end of the list "normally applies to the entire series."[15] Justice Kagan, in her dissent, relied on this practice of applying the modifier to the

---

11. George W. Bush, Address to a Joint Session of Congress (Sept. 20, 2001), in BILL ADLER, THE QUOTABLE GEORGE W. BUSH: A PORTRAIT IN HIS OWN WORDS 54, 54–55 (2004).

12. 577 U.S. 347 (2016).

13. *Id.* at 349.

14. *Id.* (quoting 18 U.S.C. § 2262(b)(2)).

15. *Id.* at 364 (Kagan, J., dissenting) (quoting ANTONIN SCALIA & BRYAN A. GARNER, READING LAW: THE INTERPRETATION OF LEGAL TEXTS 147 (2012)).

entire list in concluding that the modifier "involving a ward or minor" modified all parts of the parallel list in the statute. The majority, however, disagreed, finding that the modifier only modified the last item in the series.

Justice Sotomayor, delivering the opinion of the Court, gave this example to support her view that the last phrase only modified the last noun in the series:

> For example, imagine you are the general manager of the Yankees and you are rounding out your 2016 roster. You tell your scouts to find a defensive catcher, a quick-footed shortstop, or a pitcher from last year's World Champion Kansas City Royals. It would be natural for your scouts to confine their search for a pitcher to last year's championship team, but to look more broadly for catchers and shortstops.[16]

The dissent, however, disagreed with this example because, unlike the statute in question, the majority's hypothetical search for a player created a list that was not parallel.[17] Specifically, the dissent explained as follows:

> The words "catcher" and "shortstop," but not "pitcher," are qualified separate and apart from the modifying clause at the end of the sentence: "Pitcher" thus calls for a modifier of its own, and the phrase "from the Kansas City Royals" answers that call. Imagine the sentence is slightly reworded to refer to "a defensive catcher, quick-footed shortstop, or hard-throwing pitcher from the Kansas City Royals."... [A]ll three players must come from the Royals—because the three terms (unlike in the majority's sentence) are a parallel series with a modifying clause at the end.[18]

Therefore, even the Supreme Court cares about parallel construction.

---

16. *Id.* at 351–52.

17. *Id.* at 364 n.1 (Kagan, J., dissenting).

18. *Id.* Because I am from Kansas City, all I could focus on while reading this opinion is how thrilling it is for the Supreme Court to be discussing my Kansas City Royals.

Further, great legal writers use parallel construction in their work. Chief Justice John Roberts was one such writer before he was a Justice; in fact, he was known as one of the "best" brief writers the Justices had ever seen.[19] One of the techniques he used was parallelism. In *Alaska Department of Environmental Conservation v. EPA*, representing Red Dog Mine, Justice Roberts (then attorney Roberts) created this parallel list:

> The Red Dog Mine is the largest private employer in the Northwest Arctic Borough, where geography and the harsh environment pose unique employment challenges, offer few employment alternatives, and limit any concern about other industrial development that might compete with the mine for consumption of available increments.[20]

Note that the verbs "pose," "offer," and "limit" are all parallel.

Similarly, the Solicitor General's office recently filed a brief with the United States Supreme Court that also used parallel construction.[21] In the statement of facts, the lawyers wrote this sentence using parallel construction: "Petitioner's general practice is to **create** copyrighted designs, **print** them on fabric, and then '**market** the designed fabrics to garment manufacturers.'"[22] The bolded words are all parallel. Similarly, the lawyers wrote this about the law: "An inaccurate statement concerning the date of a work's first publication may reflect the registrant's error of law, error of fact, or both."[23] Note that the writers say, "error of law" and "error of fact" to keep them parallel.

---

19. *Write Like John Roberts, supra* note 5.

20. Brief for Petitioner at 9, Alaska Dep't of Env't Conservation v. EPA, 540 U.S. 461 (2004) (No. 02-658), 2003 WL 2010655, at *9.

21. Brief for the United States as Amicus Curiae Supporting Petitioner at 5, Unicolors, Inc. v. H&M Hennes & Mauritz, L.P., No. 20-915 (U.S. Aug. 1, 2021), 2021 WL 3633822, at *5.

22. *Id.* (emphasis added).

23. *Id.* at 13, 2021 WL 3633822, at *13.

D. How to Write Using Parallel Construction

Now that we have seen parallelism in action, here is some advice on how to make your sentences parallel. Think of the base of a sentence like the root of a tree, and then make sure the branches all match.[24] Here is an example:

> The teacher said that she was an excellent student (the root) because (the branches) she was prepared for class, she turned in her assignments on time, and she paid attention to the details of her citations.

Here is the same sentence where the branches do not match the root:

> The teacher said she was an excellent student because she was prepared for class, likes turning in her assignments on time, and pays attention to the details of her citation.

Notice that the sentence does not use parallelism; it is like writing about three different trees, and the reader is not going to feel the rhythm.

In general, the most common mistakes students make with parallelism are with lists or series, which can either be simple or more complicated.[25] Here is an example of faulty construction:

> Today, I will clean the bedroom, the living room, and wash the car.

How do you fix it? Listen to the sound of the items in a list or the items being compared. Do you hear the same kinds of sounds? Do you hear a rhythm being repeated? If something is breaking that rhythm or repetition, check to see if the construction needs to be parallel. One way to do this with items in a list is to put them in a column to see if they are parallel. Then, break down the components of the sentence and make sure they work individually before combining them.

---

24. Salmon, *supra* note 4, at 10; *see also* RAMBO & PFLAUM, *supra* note 3, at 516–19.

25. Sometimes, especially when dealing with a legal test that might be difficult to paraphrase without changing its meaning, it's not possible to achieve perfect balance. In this situation, the way to handle it is to place the longest clause in the series last, if logically possible. RAMBO & PFLAUM, *supra* note 3, at 519. That way the flow is not disrupted at the beginning.

Let's take the example above:

I will	clean the bedroom
	the living room
	wash the car

Now, let's fix it:

I will	clean the bedroom
	sweep the living room
	wash the car

Let's take a phrase:

The lawyer behaved unethically	In questioning the opposing party
	When he failed to cite adverse authorities
	And did not disclose a conflict of interest.

Let's fix it:

The lawyer behaved unethically	By questioning the opposing party
	By failing to cite to adverse authority
	By failing to disclose a conflict of interest

Let's take another example:[26]

Let's say you read a legal test that provides the situations under which a lawyer must disclose adverse authority known to the lawyer that arises from the controlling jurisdiction not already disclosed by opposing counsel. You want to turn that legal test into a list of elements, and you want that list to be parallel. How do you do it?

One way that does not work is this:

> A lawyer must disclose adverse authority that is: (1) known to him; (2) arises from the controlling jurisdiction; and (3) that was not disclosed by opposing counsel.

In the above example, there are two problems. First, the last element does not follow from the lead-in because it reads: A lawyer must disclose

---

26. This example is taken from Wayne Scheiss's blog, *Legible*. *See* Wayne Schiess, Univ. Tex. Austin Blog Serv.: Legible, *Parallelism Basics* (Feb. 12, 2015), http://sites.utexas.edu/legalwriting/2015/02/12/parallelism-basics/.

adverse authority that is "that was not disclosed by opposing counsel." This makes no sense. The second problem is that the first words of each element are not the same parts of speech. "Is" and "arises" are verbs, but "that" is a conjunction. There is a mismatch.

How do you fix the problem? One way is to repeat the word "that" each time, so it would look like this:

> A lawyer must disclose adverse authority: (1) that is known to him; (2) that arises from the controlling jurisdiction; and (3) that was not disclosed by opposing counsel.

That would result in a lot of "thats." Another way to fix it is to change the legal test, so each part begins with a verb like this:

> A lawyer must disclose adverse authority that: (1) is known to him; (2) arises from the controlling jurisdiction; and (3) was not disclosed by opposing counsel.

Let's take one last example using the legal test for restitution:

> Faulty parallelism: Restitution is recoverable only if a victim can meet three requirements: (1) economic loss; (2) the loss must be one that the victim would not have incurred but for the criminal conduct; and (3) direct causation between the criminal conduct and the economic loss.

> Corrected: To recover restitution, all the following requirements must be met: (1) the loss must be economic; (2) the loss must be one that the victim would not have incurred but for the criminal conduct; and (3) the loss must be directly caused by the criminal conduct.

Thus, because lawyers routinely use lists of items, they need to be constantly on the lookout for faulty parallel construction.

The next area of difficulty which commonly arises in legal writing is the use of correlative conjunctions. Correlative conjunctions are sort of like tag-team conjunctions.[27] They come in pairs, and you must place

---

27. Beth Parent, *Correlative Conjunctions*, YOUR DICTIONARY, https://grammar. yourdictionary.com/parts-of-speech/conjunctions/correlative-conjunctions.html

both correctly in a sentence to make them work. They get their name from the fact that they work together (con, meaning "with") and relate one sentence element to another (creating a junction). Correlative conjunctions include pairs such as "both/and," "either/or," "neither/nor," "not/but" and "not only/but also."

One way to check for parallelism is to make sure that the same part of speech follows each half of the pair.[28] The Redbook gives this example:

> We plan to either recoup our investment in the first three years
> or to sell the assets and move on.

What is the problem with that? The problem is that after "either" appears the verb "recoup" but after "or," it says, "to sell," an infinitive verb, so "recoup" and "to sell" do not match. To correct the problem, just omit the "to" before "sell." The other option is to switch the positions of "either" and the "to" before recoup and keep the "to" before "sell," like this: "We plan either to recoup our investment in the first three years or to sell the assets and move on."

Here is another example of a faulty construction using a correlative conjunction:

> Most law students are not only smart but also think creatively.[29]

Did you spot the problem? Smart is an adjective, but think is a verb. They do not match. How do you fix the problem? This is how:

> Most law students are not only smart but creative.

Therefore, with one slight change, all is right with the world, and you end up with both smart and creative law students (because they use parallel construction in their writing).

Next time you review your writing, review it for faulty parallel construction. Pay close attention to lists or series of items as well as correlative conjunctions. And always remember to stay inside the zebra crossing.

---

28. Bryan A. Garner, The Redbook: A Manual on Legal Style 237 (4th ed. 2018).

29. Schiess, *supra* note 26.

The Benefits of Active Voice

How to Write Like James Bond, the Black Panther, and Wonder Woman

....

When I practiced law for 25 years, I never gave much thought to what voice I was using because I was too busy trying to make sure my voice was being heard, period. I was taking depositions, arguing motions, fighting discovery battles, and hoping that, someday, a client would hire me. But once I started teaching legal writing, I realized that voice matters *a lot*. And, in case you are wondering, I do not mean tone, pitch, volume, or other characteristics of *spoken voice*. I mean *written voice*, where the battle line is *active vs. passive*. For those of you who like the "answer first" (you are in good company because lawyers and judges also like it when the conclusion is up front), here it is. Simply speaking, active voice is good; passive voice is bad, with some exceptions.

I also quickly saw that many students (and others) cannot recognize the difference between active and passive voice, much less fix a sentence that is passive and turn it into an active sentence. So, what is active voice and what is passive voice?

Here is an example:

Active voice: Kay steered the boat.
Passive voice: The boat was steered by Kay.

To be clear—passive voice is not grammatically incorrect.[1] As one style guide put it, "the avoidance of [active voice] is a moral failure, not

---

1. MIGNON FOGARTY, GRAMMAR GIRL'S QUICK AND DIRTY TIPS FOR BETTER WRITING 172 (2008); WILLIAM STRUNK, JR. & E. B. WHITE, THE ELEMENTS OF STYLE 18 (4th ed., Longman 1999) (stating that the rule to use active voice does not mean "the writ-

a grammatical one."[2] It's a matter of style. For example, you *can* wear brown shoes with a black dress, but should you?

Although people may have different ideas about style, the fashion police have no discretion when it comes to legal writing—active voice is the way to go. No contest. If there were an election, and active voice were running against passive voice, active voice would win in a landslide.

A. Everyone Loves Active Voice

Who would vote for active voice? Well, judges, for one, whose votes should carry significant weight.

Let's start with the United States Supreme Court, in a case where the Court essentially *blamed* passive voice for creating the problem. In *United States v. Wilson*,[3] the issue was whether the district court or the Attorney General had the authority to compute credit for time served when a defendant is sentenced. No one disputed that the defendant was entitled to credit for time spent in presentence detention before conviction, but the problem arose because Congress, in enacting the sentencing act, forgot to specify who computes the credit. Congress, writing in passive voice, provided as follows: "A defendant shall be given credit toward the service of a term of imprisonment for any time he has spent in official detention prior to the date the sentence commences."[4] The Court, critiquing Congress's use of passive voice, stated that "[w]hen Congress writes a statute in the passive voice, it often fails to indicate who must take a required action. This silence can make the meaning of a statute somewhat difficult to ascertain."[5] Ultimately, the Court held that the Attorney General had the authority.

---

er should entirely discard the passive voice, which is frequently convenient and sometimes necessary."). The term "voice" is used to refer to the quality that indicates whether the subject of the sentence is "doing the acting or receiving the acting." Laura Brown, *What's the Big Deal About the Passive Voice*, Forbes (May 20, 2019, 11:29 AM), https://www.forbes.com/sites/laurambrown/2019/05/10/whats-the-big-deal-about-the-passive-voice/?sh=1974ee6748e7.

2. Benjamin Dreyer, Dreyer's English 15 (2019).

3. 503 U.S. 329 (1992).

4. *Id.* at 332 (quoting 18 U.S.C. § 3585(b)).

5. *Id.* at 334–35.

Dissenting, Justices Stevens and White also blamed passive voice, noting that the text, "which uses the passive voice, does not specify who will make the decision about jail credit."[6] But based on that failure to specify, the dissent found that because no decisionmaker was identified, it should be interpreted as allowing either the Attorney General or the judge to make the decision, depending on the circumstances. Thus, while the Justices disagreed on the outcome, they agreed on the culprit: passive voice.

Moving down the chain of authority, in one survey, twenty-three federal appellate judges from the First, Second, and Tenth Circuits agreed that "it bothers [them] when a brief uses the passive voice frequently."[7] The Seventh Circuit has joined in this chorus, taking upon itself the task of explaining the problem with passive voice in *United States v. Torres*.[8] A drug enforcement agent stated in an affidavit that "the brown paper bag carried by [the defendant] was opened revealing a white powdery substance to the undercover agent."[9] The court, which could not tell who opened the bag because of the passive voice, criticized its use as confusing:

> Good writers eschew the passive voice not only because a sentence written passively is often not as forceful as a sentence written actively, but more importantly, because sentences written passively are more often ambiguous than those written actively. [The agent's] sentence poignantly illustrates how a passively written sentence can lead to possible confusion.[10]

Fortunately for the government in *Torres*, the court upheld the conviction despite the use of passive voice. But there are many examples of cases where passive voice impacted a party's legal rights.

---

6. *Id.* at 341–42 (Stevens, J., dissenting).

7. *See* David Lewis, *If You Have Seen One Circuit, Have You Seen Them All? A Comparison of the Advocacy Preferences of Three Federal Circuit Courts of Appeal*, 83 Denv. Univ. L. Rev. 893, 895, 906 (2006).

8. 965 F.2d 303, 310 (7th Cir. 1992).

9. *Id.* at 309.

10. *Id.* at 310.

Let's look at an example of how passive voice harmed a plaintiff's ability to even get a court to hear one of her claims.[11] In *Ponder v. County of Winnebago*, an employee sued her employer for various claims including denial of due process because she did not get a hearing before being terminated. To be denied due process, however, an employee must show that the employee had a protectible property interest in employment—in other words, a contract of employment. The defendant moved to dismiss the complaint for failure to state a claim arguing, among other things, that the plaintiff was an at-will employee who could be fired at any time without a hearing. In her complaint, the employee alleged that "[s]he was assured that she would continue on the job as long as she performed satisfactorily."[12] Blaming in part her use of passive voice, the court dismissed the due process claim because the allegation failed to give defendants notice of the claim. It emphasized that her "allegation uses the passive voice, so the Court and the defendants are left to speculate who made the assurances. Maybe we can guess that [her employer] made them, but she doesn't say."[13] Though several other claims survived the motion to dismiss, her due process claim was thrown out because her lawyer used passive voice.

Similarly, a court dismissed plaintiffs' claims for false arrest and malicious prosecution, in part, because of their use of passive voice.[14] In *Fullen v. City of Salina*, the plaintiffs alleged in their complaint that they "were arrested," "held in the Saline County jail for over 48 hours prior to being charged with multiple misdemeanors in connection with false allegations of animal cruelty," and "maliciously prosecuted at the insistence of City personnel."[15] The court held that these allegations were insufficient to state a claim, emphasizing that plaintiffs' petition was "riddled with allegations in the passive voice," and when various officials have taken different actions with respect to a plaintiff, a "plaintiff's facile, passive-voice showing that his rights 'were violated'" will not suffice.[16]

---

11. Ponder v. Cnty. of Winnebago, No. 3:20-cv-50041, 2021 WL 3269842 (N.D. Ill. Sept. 30, 2021).

12. *Id.* at *7.

13. *Id.*

14. Fullen v. City of Salina, No. 21-4010, 2021 WL 4476780, (D. Kan. Sept. 30, 2021).

15. *Id.* at *10.

16. *Id.* at *11.

Finally, the use of passive voice in drafting a contract can make it ambiguous and be held against the lawyer who drafted it.[17] In *SEC v. Mutual Benefits Corp.*, at issue was the meaning of a provision in a contract with an investor, Acheron, that provided for removal of insurance policies from a trust. The provision stated that "any policy as to which Acheron has acquired 100% of the interests may be removed from the Trust."[18] Because of the use of passive voice, the provision did not state who can do the removing, creating a dispute about which party had the right to do that. Addressing the issue, the court first stated that because the agreement failed to explicitly denote the rights of the parties, it was ambiguous, and thus, evidence outside the contract would be considered in construing it.[19] Second, the court stated that the drafter of the ambiguous provision using the passive wording should bear the adverse consequences, and thus, the provision would be interpreted against the drafter.[20] The drafter lost—and so did passive voice.

Aside from judges, who else would vote for active voice? Legal writing experts would also come out in droves to vote for active voice.[21] For example, Bryan Garner, in his style manual *The Redbook*, says that "[w]riters should watch for it and prefer the active voice unless there is good reason not to."[22] Similarly, in *Legal Writing by Design*, the authors recommend using active voice and avoiding passive voice, because passive voice weakens the "oomph" value of our sentences.[23] In *A Lawyer Writes*, the authors also recommend minimizing the passive voice so that your reader can quickly figure out who did what.[24] And finally, legal writing expert Richard Neumann and his co-authors have included a checklist in their legal writing textbook for effective style in legal writ-

---

17. SEC v. Mut. Benefits Corp., No. 04-60573-CIV, 2020 WL 5259162 (S.D. Fla. Sept. 3, 2020).

18. *Id.* at *4.

19. *Id.* at *5.

20. *Id.* at *12.

21. Judith D. Fischer, *Why George Orwell's Ideas About Language Still Matter for Lawyers*, 68 Mont. L. Rev. 129, 139 (2007).

22. Bryan A. Garner, The Redbook: A Manual on Legal Style 221 (4th ed. 2018) [hereinafter Redbook]

23. Teresa J. Reid Rambo & Leanne J. Pflaum, Legal Writing by Design 474 (2d ed. 2013).

24. Christine Coughlin et al., A Lawyer Writes 277 (3d ed. 2018).

ing, and one of those items is avoiding passive voice because it can be wordy, vague, and boring.[25]

Clients, actual and potential, whose views we care about, also prefer active voice. In an interesting empirical study, the first of its kind, a legal writing professor published the first U.S. study to measure the public's preferences for legal communication.[26] Through an online survey, clients and other members of the public were asked various questions designed to find out their thoughts about understandable communication with attorneys.[27] About 376 people responded to the survey, representing a cross-section of ages and levels of education.[28] Four of the questions were designed to find out their preferences for active vs. passive voice.[29] The online survey randomized the order of the responses, but here is an unrandomized version of those questions:

> Q. 14: The employer's attorney questioned the witnesses.
>
> The witnesses were questioned by the employer's attorney.
>
> Q. 16: The Board of Directors decided to review the file.
>
> A decision was made by the Board of Directors to review the file.
>
> Q. 22: The court dismissed the case.
>
> The case was dismissed by the court.
>
> Q. 24: Michigan courts have consistently held that homeowners must actually supply alcohol to a minor to violate the statute.
>
> It has been consistently held by Michigan courts that a homeowner must actually engage in the supplying of alcohol to a minor to commit a violation of the statute.

The participants in the study preferred the active voice 69% of the time.[30] Another interesting finding in this study was that those partici-

---

25. RICHARD K. NEUMANN ET AL., LEGAL REASONING AND LEGAL WRITING 209, 215 (Wolters Kluwer 8th ed. 2017).

26. Christopher R. Trudeau, *The Public Speaks: An Empirical Study of Legal Communication*, 14 SCRIBES J. LEGAL WRITING 121-22 (2012).

27. *Id.* at 135–49.

28. *Id.* at 134, 139.

29. *Id.* at 144.

30. *Id.* at 145.

pants who had experienced working with attorneys (and thus were more familiar with things such as legalese) opposed passive language more than those participants who were not working with attorneys. Thus, the author concluded that "this study helps dispel the notion that higher-educated people will not mind traditional legal language."[31]

So far, it looks like all the key constituents in the legal community—judges, attorneys, legal writing scholars, and even clients—would support active voice over passive voice if it were taken to a vote. But how about constituents outside the parochial enclave of the legal community? Well, it looks like passive voice has broad appeal.

George Orwell, a novelist and essayist, has been credited as having an enormous influence on the movement toward using plain English in legal writing.[32] Orwell proposed six rules of style for English writers, and the fourth rule was "[n]ever use the passive [voice] where you can use the active."[33] Similarly, Strunk & White, in *The Elements of Style*, recommend using the active voice.[34] In the *New York Times* bestseller *Dreyer's English*, readers are instructed to avoid the passive voice.[35] In *Grammar Girl*, another *New York Times* bestseller, readers are told that passive voice is awkward, vague, and wordy.[36]

B. Passive Voice Is Loved Only by Rascals

Despite this, there would be some people who would vote for passive voice. For example, a criminal defendant who is charged with stabbing someone in a bar, would probably prefer counsel use passive voice and write, "the person in the bar was stabbed" instead of using the active voice and write, "the defendant stabbed the victim in a bar."

Likewise, politicians and others would vote for passive voice because it allows them to talk about harmful actions they have taken without admitting blame. For example, if you were President Reagan, and you

---

31. *Id.* at 152.

32. Fischer, *supra* note 21, at 134.

33. George Orwell, *Politics and the English Language*, in A COLLECTION OF ESSAYS 156, 170 (Harcourt Brace Jovanovich 1993) (1946).

34. STRUNK & WHITE, *supra* note 1, at 18.

35. DREYER, *supra* note 2, at 14.

36. FOGARTY, *supra* note 1, at 171–72.

were involved in the Iran-Contra scandal, you would rather say, "serious mistakes were made," than "Sorry I sold arms to Iran and shipped the proceeds to Contras in Nicaragua without informing Congress."[37] Or, if you were Justin Timberlake, and you pulled part of Janet Jackson's bra panels off during the halftime performance of the 2004 Superbowl, you would rather say, "I am sorry if anyone was offended by the wardrobe malfunction during the halftime performance,"[38] instead of saying, "I am sorry I pulled part of Janet Jackson's bra panels off revealing a nipple on a family show like the Superbowl." (By the way, I love Justin Timberlake.) In other words, you will raise a hand for passive voice if you want to apologize without actually apologizing.

Further, when a writer wants to emphasize a result, as opposed to who did what, passive voice is appropriate.[39] For example, if you want to point out that someone was nominated to serve on a committee, you would say, "Sylvia was nominated to serve on the committee," without saying who nominated her because it does not matter. As another example, if you want to describe what was served at dinner, you might say, "Turkey, stuffing, mashed potatoes, and sweet potatoes were served." In that sentence, it does not matter who served those items but only that they were served.

If you are a legislative body, and your intent is to avoid specifying a particular actor to whom the statute's command is directed, you should use passive voice.[40] For example, if your goal is not to restrict who can sue under a statute, you will not specifically identify who can sue but use passive voice instead. For example, in *Gladstone Realtors v. Village of Bellwood*, the Court was faced with interpreting a statute that provided that "[t]he rights granted by [a related statute] ... may be enforced by

---

37. Baden Eunson, *'Mistakes Were Made': Detecting the Sneaky Passive Voice*, The Conversation (June 15, 2014, 4:34 PM), https://theconversation.com/mistakes-were-made-detecting-the-sneaky-passive-voice-27390.

38. Bethonie Butler & Elahe Izadi, *Everything You Forgot About Janet Jackson and Justin Timberlake's 2004 Super Bowl Controversy*, Wash. Post (Feb. 1, 2018), https://www.washingtonpost.com/news/arts-and-entertainment/wp/2017/10/23/everything-you-forgot-about-janet-jackson-and-justin-timberlakes-2004-super-bowl-controversy/.

39. Redbook, *supra* note 22, at 221–22.

40. *See* State v. Neff, 265 P.3d 62, 65 (Or. Ct. App. 2011).

civil actions in appropriate United States district courts."[41] Because of the use of the passive voice, the statute did not specify who could enforce the rights the statute granted. Ultimately, the Court explained that because there were no restrictions on plaintiffs who could sue, Congress did not intend to restrict access to the federal courts to a specific class of plaintiffs.[42]

Finally, when someone simply does not know who did the acting, passive voice is appropriate. Let's say you leave your laptop in a restaurant, and when you return a day later, it's gone. You would say, "it was stolen." You have no idea who took it, so passive voice is appropriate. Or you come from a big family with many siblings, and you put your leftovers in the refrigerator, but they are gone the next morning. You will say, "my leftovers are gone," because you don't know which one of your siblings took them. That is, unless you know that one of them is guilty, in which case you will of course use active voice and specify the culprit loudly and clearly.

C. A Brief and Clear Case for Active Voice

So, judges, clients, and legal writing experts all prefer active voice—and people who prefer passive voice are probably trying to avoid the blame for stealing leftovers or for funding right-wing rebel groups in Latin America. Not using active voice when you should might have serious consequences. And there are really only a few situations where passive voice is acceptable. It's clear that active voice has a lot going for it; still, in every election the candidates need a clear platform. What would active voice's platform be? Active voice would argue that its use promotes clarity and brevity, two core goals in legal writing. I see the campaign poster now:

Voting for Me as Easy as ABC
Active voice means
Brevity and
Clarity

---

41. 441 U.S. 91, 102–03 (1979) (quoting 42 U.S.C. § 3612 (1976) (repealed 1988)).
42. *Id.* at 102–09.

As far as brevity, all we need to do is to consider the examples from the empirical study discussed above to see that using active voice will save on words. Consider this example, which was part of the study:

Option One — Active Voice: The court dismissed the case.

Option Two — Passive Voice: The case was dismissed by the court.

The active voice option is five words; the passive voice option is seven words—a savings of two words. Now, you might be thinking, in the scheme of things, who cares if I save two words? You do for several reasons. First, no one wants to read your writing.[43] Say that again? That's correct. People read your writing because they must and not because they really want to. It's not like grabbing the latest John Grisham novel off the shelf and bringing it to the beach for a pleasure read. Legal writing (and reading) is not like that, so you can do your audience a favor by giving the audience less to read. As one federal district judge put it when writing about the "writer-reader contract," because the contract requires valuing the reader's time, "it's best honored with overall brevity...."[44]

Second, brevity promotes clarity, the chief hallmark of good legal writing.[45]

Third, there are practical reasons to use fewer words: as a lawyer and even as a law student, you will be up against strict word limits. As a lawyer, you will spend much of your time looking for places to cut words. In fact, when I was a lawyer (a litigator—bringing and defending cases in court), if someone had asked, "What are you doing all day?" I would say, "mainly looking for places to omit needless words."

If you do not believe me about strict word counts, let me give you some examples. The Seventh Circuit Court of Appeals struck a party's brief (in other words, the court would not read it and ordered him to file another brief within the word count) because the party told the court that his brief was fewer than 14,000 words, but the brief was actually over

---

43. Zeb Landsman, No One Wants to Read Your Brief 1 (2021).

44. Andrew J. Guilford, *Legal Writing: a Contract Between the Reader and the Writer*, Cal. Bar J., https://www.calbarjournal.com/November2010/TopHeadlines/TH4.aspx (last visited Jan. 11, 2022).

45. Mark Osbeck, *What Is "Good Legal Writing" and Why Does It Matter?*, 4 Drexel L. Rev. 417, 427, 438 (2012).

16,000 words.[46] The party argued that he did not think the word count included such things as footnotes or citations to the law. The court rejected this argument, stating that these count under the applicable rule.[47]

Likewise, the United States Court of Appeals for the Federal Circuit dismissed a party's appeal when the party failed to comply with the 14,000 word limit.[48] Specifically, the party squeezed various words together and eliminated spaces to limit words. Although the party filed a corrected brief, the party engaged in similar underhanded practices, such as using odd abbreviations, making the brief nearly incomprehensible. After giving that side of the case two chances to get within the word count—chances the party squandered—the court went so far as to dismiss the appeal.

So does eliminating two words make a difference? It could.

D. How Passive Voice Can Be Fixed by Zombies

Now that we have made a compelling case for active voice, what do we do about those passive-voice loyalists reluctant to change? Can we give them a path to redemption? Can we show them how they can convert from passive to active voice? We must. So let's learn how to identify passive voice and fix it.

The passive voice consists of a *be*-verb combined with the past participle of a transitive verb.[49] If that doesn't help clarify the matter, you are not alone. I like this explanation better: When active voice is used, the subject is doing the acting, but in passive voice, the target of the action gets promoted to the subject position.[50]

For example, take these two sentences:

1. The bicycle was pedaled by Pearl.
2. Pearl pedaled the bicycle.

---

46. Vermillion v. Corizon Health, Inc., 906 F.3d 696, 696 (7th Cir. 2018).

47. *Id.* at 697.

48. Pi-Net Int'l, Inc. v. JP Morgan Chase & Co., 600 F. App'x 774, 774–75 (Fed. Cir. 2015).

49. Redbook, *supra* note 22, at 221.

50. Fogarty, *supra* note 1, at 171.

The first example is passive voice because the target of the action—the bicycle—got a promotion to the subject position. The second example is active voice because Pearl, who is the actual subject, is doing the pedaling.

Here is another example of passive voice where the subject is unnamed, and thus it is written in passive voice:

> The car was driven.

But are there any rules of thumb or other methods I can apply to identify passive voice?[51]

One straightforward way of identifying potential passive voice is if you see a "by" in the sentence, as in, "The sword was wielded by Wonder Woman." However, that rule doesn't always work because sometimes a sentence contains the word by, and it's not in passive voice, such as, "Wonder Woman left her sword by the castle exit."

Or you can ask yourself whether you can add the words "by zombies" at the end of it.[52] Take this example:

> Contracts were entered into.

Does that sentence tell you who entered into the contracts? No. Could you add "by zombies" at the end of it? Yes. Therefore, that is passive voice.

Another way of recognizing passive voice is to ask yourself whether James Bond, Wonder Woman, or the Black Panther would say it that

---

51. One way to identify passive voice is to use a feature in Microsoft Word to help you. You can configure the word-proofing options to check for passive sentences. If you do that, a blue squiggle will appear under sentences using passive voice. Some versions will underline passive verbs in green. Word can also show you the percentage of passive sentences in your document after each spell check. The problem is that these methods are not foolproof, and Word will not always give you options to fix the problem but just tells you there is a problem. For further guidance, you can read one of the many short articles on the internet addressing how to set this feature up in Word. *E.g.*, Tammy Columbo, *How to Use Microsoft Word to Find Passive Verb Forms*, Hous. CHRON., https://smallbusiness.chron.com/use-microsoft-word-passive-verb-forms-75444.html (last visited Jan. 11, 2022); Tracy Strike, *Three Free Tools to Check Your Writing Quickly*, SPARK CONTENT (APR. 22, 2016), https://sparkcontent.ca/2016/04/22/three-free-tools-quickly-check-writing/; *Check Passive Verbs with Word and Outlook*, CLARIFYNow, https://clarifynow.co.uk/check-passive-verbs-with-word-and-outlook/ (last visited Jan. 11, 2022).

52. DREYER, *supra* note 2, at 14.

"Get the director over here. I would never say, 'He was defeated by me.'"

way. In other words, if you were an action hero, and all you did was act, would you say it that way? Find the agent, subject, or action hero in the sentence—figure out who or what is performing the act expressed in the verb and make that the subject of the sentence. You then may need to change the verb accordingly.

Here's an example:

> Gods and superheroes were attacked by Diana's weapons of vengeance.

In this sentence, the action hero, Diana (weirdly the same name of both the author and Wonder Woman), is not doing anything but instead things are being done to her. She would never put up with that. Therefore, you need to change the sentence so that she is doing the acting:

> Diana attacked the gods and superheroes with her weapons of vengeance.

Now, I know what you are thinking. You are thinking that the chances of writing about the Black Panther, Wonder Woman, or James Bond when you write about the law are slim because they are fictional characters, so these examples may not be that relevant. I agree, so to show you what passive voice looks like and how to correct it, here are some examples of sentences my students have drafted over the years:

Passive Voice Example	Identifying the Problem	Fixing It
She was awakened two hours later.	She was awakened by zombies?	Police woke her up two hours later (she was sleeping in her car because she was intoxicated).
He was never paid by his employer for writing the book.	The employer is the subject, but it is not the do-er in the sentence.	The employer never paid him for writing the book.
The book was not created by him during working hours.	The subject—the him in the sentence—is doing the acting but is being acted upon instead.	He did not create the book during working hours.
The plaintiff was discouraged from writing the book by his supervisor.	The subject—the supervisor—is doing the acting but is being acted upon instead.	His supervisor discouraged him from writing the book.
The key was kept in a lockbox.	The key was kept there by zombies?	Mr. ____ (the fictional party in the hypothetical) put the key in a lockbox.
The car he was driving was given to him by his parents.	The subject—his parents—are doing the acting but are being acted upon in this sentence.	His parents gave him the car he was driving.
The car was not furnished to him by the defendants.	The subject—the defendants—are doing the acting but are being acted upon in this sentence.	The defendants did not furnish the car to him.

In conclusion, try to stick to active voice unless you have a good reason to use passive voice. Active voice will help your writing be brief and clear, two fundamental goals in legal writing.

"Now where do we go?"

Your Writing Should Not Feel Like Riding in an ATV

Transitions Can Smooth the Path

O ne area that I find students pay little attention to is the transitions they use in their writing. Sometimes the problem is not including a transition, sometimes the problem is using the wrong transition, and sometimes it is both. Transitions are a topic near and dear to my heart, prompting me to speak and write on this topic frequently.[1]

Transitions are one of the keys to "flow" in legal writing.[2] They allow your reader to move seamlessly from one idea to another. As I often say to my students, "While you might see the connection between your ideas, your reader might not be able to, so you need to be transparent about showing that relationship to your reader through your transitions." In this chapter, we will cover what transitions are, the science behind the use of transitions in writing, and the "art" of using them to improve your writing.

A. What Is a Transition?

What do I mean by "transitions"? As used in this chapter, I am thinking of the broadest use of that term. It can include transitional words that most of us think of, such as *in contrast, however, similarly, further,*

---

1. Much of the information contained in this chapter on transitions comes from an article I wrote for Legal Communication & Rhetoric: JALWD. *See* Diana J. Simon, *The Power of Connectivity: The Science and Art of Transitions*, 10 Legal Comm. & Rhetoric: JALWD 65, 65–80 (2021); *See also* Diana Simon, *The Science and Art of Transitions*, Ariz. Att'y, Apr. 2018, at 12.

2. Christine Coughlin et al., A lawyer Writes 268 (3d ed. 2018).

and *for example*. But it also includes words that you might not think of as transitions, such as *and, because, including,* and *so.* Transitions can also include point headings, because, after all, they transition the reader from topic to topic. There are also a great many other words or phrases that can function as transitions depending on their specific use in a sentence. So, think broadly, but use them. If you want to see one of the more thorough lists of transitions, legal writing expert Ross Guberman has listed more than 90 transition words and phrases on his blog.[3]

B. The Science Behind Transitions

Because students tend to be skeptical about the importance of transitions, I should let you know that science is on my side: using transitions can speed reading times and improve comprehension. While you have been busy reading your casebooks, psycholinguists and cognitive psychologists, among others, have been studying the effects of "connectives"[4] on comprehension and reading times.[5] Indeed, the literature reveals that the use of transitions improves processing time and assists in comprehension. When you become a lawyer, and your job is to convince

---

3. Ross Guberman, *90 Transition Words and Phrases*, Legal Writing Pro, https://legalwritingpro.com/pdf/transition-words.pdf (last visited Mar. 17, 2022).

4. Scientists use the word "connectives"; legal writers use the word "transitions." *Compare, e.g.*, Keith K. Millis & Marcel A. Just, *The Influence of Connectives on Sentence Comprehension*, 33 J. Memory & Language 128, 128–29 (1994) (using the word "connective" to refer to the word "because"), *and* Judith Kamalski, et al., *Effects of Coherence Marking on the Comprehension and Appraisal of Discourse*, 28 J. Proc. Ann. Meeting Cognitive Sci. Soc'y (2006), https://escholarship.org/uc/item/5wn702rx (referring to the importance of connectives such as "because" and "therefore"), *with* Coughlin et al., *supra* note 2, at 271 (listing "because" as a transition) (citation omitted). *But see* Bryan A. Garner, The Redbook: A Manual on Legal Style 235 (4th ed. 2018) (defining a conjunction as joining "two or more words, phrases, clauses, or sentences" and listing "because" as a subordinating conjunction that shows a logical connection to the main clause). Interestingly, however, Garner has also referred to transition words and phrases as "explicit connectives." Bryan A. Garner, Legal Writing in Plain English 67–68 (2001).

5. *See generally* Jean Caron et al., *Conjunctions and the Recall of Composite Sentences*, 27 J. Memory & Language 309 (1988); Kamalski et al., *supra* note 4; Millis & Just, *supra* note 4; Ted J. M. Sanders & Leo G. M. Noordman, *The Role of Coherence Relations and Their Linguistic Markers in Text Processing*, 29 Discourse Processes 37 (2000); Jan H. Spyridakis & Timothy C. Standal, *Signals in Expository Prose: Effects on Reading Comprehension*, 22 Reading Rsch. Q. 285 (1987).

a judge that an argument should be adopted, having a judge understand and process the information quickly is one of your main goals.[6]

For example, in one study, the authors found that two sentences that were connected to each other using the word "because" led to faster recognition times than the same two sentences without that word.[7] The experiment was designed to test aspects of the "Connective Integration Model."[8] Under this model, when there are two clauses of a sentence connected by a word like "because," the reader first places the first clause in working memory. When the reader encounters the word connecting the clauses, the reader knows the clauses must be integrated. When the reader then reads the second clause and puts that in the reader's memory, the reader then combines both clauses into an integrated representation. If there is no connecting word, however, there is no explicit cue to integrate the statements, leading to a possible inability to integrate and comprehend the two clauses.

In one of three experiments, subjects read two pairs of statements—one pair not joined by a transition and another pair joined by the word "because." The sentence pairs were all the same length; the only difference was in the use of the connecting word.[9] Here is an example:

> Version One: The elderly parents toasted their only daughter at the party. Jill had finally passed the exams at the prestigious university.

---

6. At first blush, it might seem like the less time and effort it takes to read something, the less the reader will absorb the information. The opposite is true. "Relevance theory" is a theory that posits that perceptions of relevance vary with effort, and if more effort (and, in theory, time) is taken to process information, the reader will find the information less relevant and less worthy of attention. Elizabeth R. Baldwin, *Beyond Contrastive Rhetoric: Helping International Lawyers Use Cohesive Devices in U.S. Legal Writing*, 26 Fla. J. Int'l L. 399, 424 (2014). In contrast, if information is easy to interpret, that information has an "initial degree of plausibility." *Id.* (citation omitted).

7. Millis & Just, *supra* note 4, at 134.

8. *Id.* at 129.

9. *Id.* at 131.

Version Two: The elderly parents toasted their only daughter at the party because Jill passed the exams at the prestigious university.[10]

In each sentence pair, the first statement of the pair conveyed a possible consequence of the action or event expressed in the second statement. The subjects were provided with 72 pairs of sentences. The subjects were presented with the sentence pairs on a fast-moving computer screen, and then a "probe word" would appear; in the example above, the probe word would have been the word "toasted." They were then told to press "true" if the word had appeared in the sentence pairs and "false" if it had not. The authors of the study then measured word reading times, probe word recognition times, and the time to answer.[11] Timing was measured in milliseconds.[12]

The versions of the statements with the word "because" led to faster recognition times of the probe word than the statements without that connection.[13] In addition to being faster, the answers were more accurate.

Unlike the study above where the researchers used *related* sentences, in another experiment the researchers used *unrelated* sentence pairs to assess recall performance. In this experiment, they compared performance across a variety of different conjunctions, such as "because" and "and," that were inserted between the two clauses.[14] They also studied sentence pairs without any connection. In all cases, the sentences had a single subject and predicate and were in past tense.[15] Subjects were provided with a booklet of the sentence pairs, one pair on each page, and were told to turn the page every 7.5 seconds.[16] Subsequently, they were told to write down what they could remember of the second clause

---

10. *Id.*

11. *Id.* at 132.

12. *Id.* While the difference of a few milliseconds might not seem significant for lawyers (or any other person for that matter), in this area of research, that is the unit of measurement.

13. *Id.* at 134.

14. Caron et al., *supra* note 5, at 311.

15. *See id.*

16. *Id.* at 312.

or sentence. Recall performance was better when the sentences were connected by "because" than it was when "and" connected the sentences or there was no connecting word at all.[17]

Finally, when scientists studied the impact of transitions on readers' comprehension of longer passages, they found that when transitions were added, students scored higher on tests designed to test their understanding of the materials.[18] The materials consisted of four essays on technical topics, such as nitrates, corrosion, and algae control.[19] After reading the passages, students took a ten-question multiple-choice test.[20] Although the results were dependent on the content of the material, the use of the transitions helped readers "retain more... content and make inferences from that content."[21] The authors thus concluded that "logical connectives" appear to aid readers in understanding "expository prose."[22]

Thus, there is a scientific basis for using transitions in writing, as they improve processing times and comprehension. And some transitions work better than others.

---

17. *Id.* at 315. Similarly, in a study comparing a "problem-solution" format with a "list relation," the authors found that the problem-solution format caused a stronger link in the representation than a list structure. Sanders & Noordman, *supra* note 5, at 51.

18. Spyridakis & Standal, *supra* note 5, at 290–92. This study used multiple methods to help signal or preview comprehension: headings, previews of the material, and "logical connectives" in the form of transitions such as "for example," "therefore," "also," "additionally," and "in the meantime." *Id.* at 288–89. Because the focus of this article is on transitions, only that part of the study is addressed.

19. *Id.* at 288.

20. *Id.* at 289.

21. *Id.* at 292. In one passage that was long and at a relatively low reading level (Grade 9), the signals used had less value, leading the authors to conclude that if the passage is easy enough to understand, signals may be of less value. *Id.* at 293.

22. *Id.*

C. Transitions in Legal Writing

Transitions have been categorized into two species: *linking* transitions and *substantive* transitions.[23] A linking transition links one thought to the next and shows a causal relationship.[24] On the other hand, substantive transitions are substantive links between ideas.[25]

1. Linking Transitions

Let's first discuss linking transitions because they are easier to understand. Linking transitions like "because" and "therefore" are commonly used to connect two thoughts.[26] Other transitions, such as "further," "in contrast," or "for example," are used to advance or move a discussion forward. And words such as "first," "second," and "third" are used to connect multiple thoughts through sequence.

Let's see some in action in a real brief filed in the United States Supreme Court.[27] Here are three thesis sentences at the beginning of three sequential paragraphs in the brief:

> First thesis sentence: That categorical rule also could undermine schools' efforts to combat harassment, bullying, and other similar harms.

> Second thesis sentence: *For example*, school districts may under certain circumstances be held liable for damages if they are "deliberately indifferent to [student harassment]...."

> Third thesis sentence: *Similarly*, the Department of Education has explained that harassment and bullying of a student with a disability on any basis can rise to the level of denying a free appropriate public education....

---

23. Teresa J. Reid Rambo & Leanne J. Pflaum, Legal Writing by Design 221–25 (2d ed. 2013).

24. *Id.* at 222.

25. *Id.* at 225.

26. *Id.* at 222.

27. These examples are taken from Brief for United States as Amicus Curiae Supporting Petitioner at 16–17, Mahanoy Sch. Dist. v. B.L., 141 S. Ct. 2038 (2021) (No. 20-255), 2021 WL 859695, at *16–17.

Note that the second and third thesis sentences both begin with transitions, thereby connecting each to the subject matter above. Rather than being left in suspense, the reader understands immediately the relationship between the ideas in the last two paragraphs—one is providing an example of the thesis from the first paragraph, and the next thesis sentence informs the reader that its idea is similar to the one in the preceding paragraph. Simple, right? Your reader should not have to read on too far to figure out what the relationship is between two paragraphs (or even two sentences). You should make that relationship transparent, and you do this with linking transitions.

2. Substantive Transitions

Next, we are going to cover substantive transitions. Legal writers love these, as demonstrated by the nicknames legal writers have attached to them, such as the "Golden Gate Bridge,"[28] the "heavy-lifters" of transitions, and "dovetailing transitions."[29]

Substantive transitions have been called dovetail transitions because carpenters use dovetail joints to fasten wood without nails or screws, allowing them to fit together seamlessly, just like a substantive transition is designed to hold ideas together seamlessly.[30] Dovetailing is a strategy used often in legal writing; it is a method of joining "old information" in a sentence to "new information" that follows.[31]

To break this down for you even more, essentially there are three basic categories of substantive transitions: (1) the "repetition" transition; (2) the "restatement" transition; and (3) the "roadmap" transition.[32] Let's take each of these in turn.

a. The Repetition Transition

A repetition transition simply repeats a word or words from a prior sentence. The "repeated words are, in effect, a step backward to move

---

28. Rambo & Pflaum, *supra* note 23, at 225.

29. Tenielle Fordyce-Ruff, *Connections Count Part II; Orienting and Substantive Transitions*, Advocate, Sept. 2017, at 48, 48.

30. Anne Enquist, *Dovetailing: The Key to 'Flow' in Legal Writing*, Second Draft, Nov. 1992, at 3, 7; Fordyce-Ruff, *supra* note 29, at 48.

31. Enquist, *supra* note 30, at 3.

32. Rambo & Pflaum, *supra* note 23, at 225–29.

two steps forward."[33] To demonstrate how this works, let's take two examples—one pair of sentences that does not use a repetition transition and one that does. Which one has better flow?

> Example with no transition:
> This Court has long emphasized the "high degree of deference" that should be afforded to such judgments. Respondents seek evidence to furnish to foreign prosecutors for use in a foreign criminal investigation probing alleged clandestine CIA intelligence activity abroad.[34]

> Example with a repetition transition:
> This Court has long emphasized the *"high degree of deference"* that should be afforded to such judgments. *And the need for deference* is even greater here because respondents seek evidence to furnish to foreign prosecutors for use in a foreign criminal investigation probing alleged clandestine CIA intelligence activity abroad.

In the first example, the reader is left wondering what the second sentence—about the evidence being sought—has to do with the first sentence—relating to a high degree of deference. Therefore, the reader is momentarily disoriented and has reached a bump in the road. In the second example, with the repetition of the word "deference," the reader now gets it: the relationship between the legal standard and the type of evidence at issue in the case.

b. The Restatement Transition

The restatement transition, instead of repeating information, puts an idea in a similar light.[35] For example, here is this example of a restate-

---

33. Kenneth F. Oettle, *Transition by Repetition: Take One Step Back to Go Two Steps Forward*, MICH. BAR J., Sept. 2008, at 44, 44.

34. These statements (although edited to take out the repetition transition in the first example) are taken from the Reply Brief for the United States at 7, United States v. Zubaydah, 142 S. Ct. 959 (2022) (No. 20-827), 2017 WL 11634969, at *7.

35. RAMBO & PFLAUM, *supra* note 23, at 228.

ment transition from a case illustration involving the sufficiency of a notice of claim against a public entity:[36]

> The claimant also demanded "[a]ll economic damages... [of] approximately $35,000.00 per year or more going forward over the next 18 years" and "[g]eneral damages... in an amount of no less than $200,000.00."
>
> Based upon the claimant's *use of qualifying language*, the Court concluded that the claimant failed to identify any specific amount.

The phrase "use of qualifying language" is a concise restatement of the specific words—"approximately" and "no less than"—in the claim letter which led the Court to its conclusion.

c. The Roadmap Transition

The final category of substantive transition is the roadmap transition, which is used to introduce an idea or alert the reader to a shift in thought, such as in this example:

> Arguing that a jury that acquits on some counts while inexplicably hanging on others is not rational, the Government contends that issue preclusion is as inappropriate in this case as it was in *Powell*. *There are two serious flaws in this reasoning.*[37]

In the above example, taken from a Supreme Court opinion, the Court is alerting the reader that it is shifting from a statement about a party's position to the Court's view of that position.

In the next example, the roadmap transition is used to alert the reader to a shift from a discussion of the law to a discussion of the application of the law to the facts of the case at hand.

> In *Powell* and, before that, in *Dunn*,... we were faced with jury verdicts that, on their face, were logically inconsistent and yet we refused to impugn the legitimacy of either verdict. *In this*

---

36. This case illustration is of Deer Valley Unified Sch. Dist. No. 97 v. Houser, 152 P.3d 490, 491–93 (Ariz. 2007).

37. Yeager v. United States, 557 U.S. 110, 124 (2009) (emphasis added).

case, there is merely a suggestion that the jury may have acted irrationally.[38]

Therefore, when you think about how to connect ideas to each other, you have many tools in your toolbox to help you with that.

3. The Magic of Three — Sequencing Using First, Second, and Third

Since this chapter is about transitions, let me shift your thoughts from linking and dovetail transitions to the magic of three.

There seems to be some magic associated with the number three when advocating,[39] and interestingly, the magic of three is a recurring theme in culture in general.[40] From the story of "Goldilocks and the Three Bears," to ad slogans such as "snap, crackle, and pop," to the Holy

---

38. *Id.* at 125 (emphasis altered).

39. *See* Patrick Barry, *The Rule of Three*, 15 LEGAL COMM. & RHETORIC: JALWD 247, 247–48 (2018) ("Judges use the Rule of Three. Practitioners use the Rule of Three. And so do all manner of legal academics"); Bryan A. Garner, *Good Headings Show You've Thought Out Your Arguments Well in Advance*, ABA J. (Sept. 1, 2015, 6:00 AM), https://www.aba-journal.com/magazine/article/good_headings_show_youve_thought_out_your_arguments_well_in_advance/ ("Arguments come in threes. A mathematician once told me that there are really only four numbers in the world: one, two, three and many."); *see generally* Suzanne B. Shu & Kurt A. Carlson, *When Three Charms but Four Alarms: Identifying the Optimal Number of Claims in Persuasion Settings*, 78 J. MKTG. 127 (2014).

40. *E.g.*, DAVID TROTTIER, THE SCREENWRITER'S BIBLE 5–9 (Silman-James Press 1998); Kurt A. Carlson & Suzanne B. Shu, *The Rule of Three: How the Third Event Signals the Emergence of a Streak*, 104 ORGANIZATIONAL BEHAV. & HUM. DECISION PROCESSES 113 (2007); Andy Newman, *Blessed in Triplicate*, N.Y. TIMES (Oct. 10, 2008), https://www.nytimes.com/2008/10/12/fashion/sundaystyles/12three.html; *Three-act Structure*, WIKI-PEDIA, https://en.wikipedia.org/wiki/Three-act_structure (last visited Apr. 8, 2022). In an interview that Bryan Garner conducted of writer David Foster Wallace about how to argue persuasively, Mr. Wallace referenced the three-part structure of argumentative writing as "three tragic acts." Bryan A. Garner, *David Foster Wallace's Advice on Arguing Persuasively*, ABA J. (Dec. 1, 2013, 9:20 AM), https://www.abajournal.com/magazine/article/david_fos-ter_wallace_gives_advice_on_arguing_persuasively.

Trinity, to lucky number three,[41] to "life, liberty, and the pursuit of happiness,"[42] the number three is magical.[43]

But the impact of three is not just magic; it is actually backed by science, which has shown the number three to be important in "human learning and cognition."[44] For example, studies have shown that when learning a new word, people can generalize its definition to new objects after three examples of the word.[45] As another example, in an interesting study on persuasion in marketing messages, the authors concluded that three is optimal, while four is less positive in persuading.[46] In one of the experiments, the authors studied the relationship between the number of positive claims made about a person and the impression others had about that person.[47] In that experiment, a friend was talking up her rekindled relationship with an old boyfriend.[48] Each message had as few as one or as many as six reasons to buy in to the rekindled relationship.[49] On the four reasons scenario, the hypothetical friend says, about her old boyfriend, "He's intelligent, kind, funny, and cute."[50] At the fourth word, the subjects' eyebrows popped upward, indicating their skepti-

---

41. In China, three is a lucky number because it sounds like the word that means life, while the word four is unlucky because it sounds like the word for death. Newman, *supra* note 40.

42. Interestingly, although the first draft of the Declaration of Independence was heavily edited, no one ever tried to rework those words, sticking to the "Rule of Three." Barry, *supra* note 39, at 252.

43. *See, e.g.,* Marie D. Jones, *3: The Perfect Number—Trinity Symbolism in World Religious Traditions*, ANCIENT ORIGINS (Sept. 22, 2021), https://www.ancient-origins.net/human-origins-religions/3-perfect-number-trinity-symbolism-world-religious-traditions-005411; Newman, *supra* note 40.

44. Carlson & Shu, *supra* note 40, at 114, 120 (finding that the "third repeat event in a sequence is pivotal to the subjective belief that a streak has emerged"); Shu & Carlson, *supra* note 39, at 137 (finding that impressions conformed to the "charm of three" because consumers viewed three claims as positive but four or more as less positive).

45. Shu & Carlson, *supra* note 39 at 129 (citing J.B. Tenenbaum & F. Xu, *Word Learning as Bayesian Inference*, 114 PSYCH. REV. 245, 245–72 (2000)).

46. *Id.* at 137–38.

47. *Id.* at 130.

48. Susannah Jacob, *The Power of Three*, N.Y. TIMES (Jan. 3, 2014), https://www.nytimes.com/2014/01/05/fashion/Three-Persuasion-The-Power-of-Three.html; Shu & Carlson, *supra* note 39.

49. Jacob, *supra* note 48.

50. *Id.*

cism. Given four reasons, the subjects were more likely to answer that the friend was "kidding herself about how great John is," than they were to conclude, at three reasons, that "John is a real catch."[51] Based on this and other experiments in the study, the authors consistently found that when making positive claims, "the optimal number of claims is three, a result we refer to as the charm of three."[52] Of course, advertisers are not bound by the same code of ethics as lawyers trying to persuade a court, but the same techniques can be used to persuade.

The magic of three, reflected in the use of *first*, *second*, and *third*, is a powerful and prevalent transitional device used in legal writing by judges and lawyers alike. One recent example is *Nielsen v. Preap*,[53] a Supreme Court case dealing with the detention of legal immigrants with criminal histories, where the device appears in both the concurring and dissenting opinions.[54] The Court ruled that the government has the power to detain immigrants at any time that have committed certain crimes that could lead to their deportation, even if those crimes occurred long in the past.[55] Interestingly, in the majority opinion, the Justices use the transition "first" in two different parts of the opinion but never follow that up with a second or third.[56] In their concurrence, however, Justices Thomas and Gorsuch use first, second, and third as a means to transition their points.[57] Below are the statements which include the transitions:

> First, [the statute] bars judicial review of "all questions of law and fact . . ."
>
> Second, [the statute] provides that "[n]o court may set aside any action or decision . . . under this section . . . ."

---

51. *Id.*

52. Shu & Carlson, *supra* note 39, at 138.

53. 139 S. Ct. 954 (2019); *see also, e.g.*, Dep't of Rev. v. Ass'n of Wash. Stevedoring Cos., 435 U.S. 734, 746–47 (1978) (noting that "[f]irst *Puget Sound* invalidated the Washington tax on stevedoring," "[s]econd," *Carter & Weekes* supported its reaffirmance of *Puget Sound*, and "[t]hird," *Carter & Weekes* reaffirmed *Puget Sound*).

54. *Nielsen*, 139 S. Ct. at 964, 974.

55. *See id.* at 959.

56. *Id.* at 964, 969.

57. *Id.* at 974–75 (Thomas, J., concurring in part).

Third, [the statute] deprives district courts of "jurisdiction or authority to enjoin or restrain the operation of [the statute]....."[58]

Similarly, Justices Breyer, Ginsburg, Sotomayor, and Kagan, who dissented, not only used these linking transitions, but they also emphasized them with italics as follows:

First, "Congress often drafts statutes with hierarchical schemes...."

Second, consider the structural similarities between [subsections]....

Third, Congress' enactment of a special "transition" statute strengthens the point.[59]

Likewise, in dissent in *Parents Involved in Community Schools v. Seattle School District No. 1,*[60] Justices Breyer, Stevens, Souter, and Ginsburg also used only the three linking transitions:

First, there is a historical and remedial element: an interest in setting right the consequences of prior conditions of segregation.

Second, there is an educational element: an interest in overcoming the adverse educational effects produced by and associated with highly segregated schools.

Third, there is a democratic element: an interest in producing an educational environment that reflects the "pluralistic society" in which our children will live.[61]

This pattern is not limited to judicial opinions. Brief writers also follow this pattern. For example, in a brief co-authored by the Attorney General

---

58. *Id.*

59. *Id.* at 980–81 (Breyer, J., dissenting) (emphasis in original).

60. 551 U.S. 701 (2007).

61. *Id.* at 838–40 (Breyer, J., dissenting).

and Solicitor General for the State of Vermont submitted to the Supreme Court, the three linking transitions are used as follows:[62]

> First, and crucially, the Solicitor General recognizes that "the Vermont reporting requirements" have "an entirely different focus" from ERISA's ... requirements.

> Second, the Solicitor General agrees that the "mere fact that a state-law reporting obligation encompasses information about the operation of an ERISA plan does not suffice for preemption."

> Third, the Solicitor General, like the dissenting judge below, finds no basis in this record to hold that Vermont's law is preempted.[63]

Thus, if you can distill your arguments down to three main points, use first, second, and third.

In sum, when someone reads your writing, the journey should not feel like riding a mountain bike, sitting in one of those jeeps on some

---

62. Supplemental Brief for Petitioner at 4–5, Gobeille v. Liberty Mut. Ins. Co., 557 U.S. 312 (2016), 2015 WL 3486603, at *4–5 [hereinafter *Gobeille*]; *see also* Supplemental Brief for Petitioner at 3–4, CMC Heartland Partners v. Union Pac. R.R., 519 U.S. 1090 (1997), 1997 WL 33557885, at *3–4 (using first, second, and third as linking transitions). Interestingly, this use of three points seems to extend to advice given on oral arguments at well. *See* Mike Skotnicki, *Make Your Argument Stronger with the "Power of Three,"* Brief-ly Writing (Dec. 5, 2013), https://brieflywriting.com/2013/12/05/make-your-argument-stronger-with-the-power-of-three/ (noting that "the human mind quickly recalls no more than three things from a list," and so when making oral arguments to a court, make sure to include only three arguments or reasons for the ruling); *Tips on Oral Advocacy*, Duke L., https://law.duke.edu/life/mootcourt/tips/ (last visited Apr. 8, 2022) (instructing moot court participants to identify two or three but *no more than three* issues to discuss). Similarly, when Bryan Garner wrote an article giving advice on persuasive point headings, he recommended that advocates try to distill arguments down to three main points. Bryan A. Garner, *Good Headings Show You've Thought out Your Arguments Well in Advance*, ABA J. (Sept. 1, 2015, 6:00 AM), https://www.abajournal.com/magazine/article/good_headings_show_youve_thought_out_your_arguments_well_in_advance/ ("Arguments come in threes.... A mathematician once told me that there are really only four numbers in the world: one, two, three and many."). Obviously, however, it is not always possible to make three main points. If a claim has only two elements or has four elements, as examples, there would probably be no reason to divide those arguments into three parts.

63. *Gobeille, supra* note 62, at *4–5.

extreme off-road adventure, or toughing it out while on one of those herky-jerky rides in an amusement park. Think calm, smooth waters, and use transitions to help with the flow.

"Actually, I'm waiting on one more."

13

Explanatory Parentheticals

The Short Stories of Legal Writing

B efore getting into parentheticals, I want to tell you about my dog. My friend found him abandoned under a car when he was only 10 weeks old, so we took him in. The first thing we did was sign up for puppy school, where he learned about 15 commands. He is now seven years old, and he only knows about five of those commands. (This is my fault for not continually reinforcing the other 10 commands, so please do not blame my dog or think he does not have the brains to retain all commands because he is, of course, brilliant.) Of the commands he learned, the two most important ones are "stay" and "leave it." "Stay" is critical because if he did not stay when I walked down our driveway to fetch the mail, he could run out in the street. "Leave it" is just as critical because he puts everything in his mouth, including whatever crumbs might be left on the floor, so if he did not obey, he could ingest something (like chocolate) that could hurt him. You are wondering what this has to do with explanatory parentheticals. Bear with me.

Those 15 commands my dog learned in puppy school are like all the things you are learning about in law school. Not everything is critical; some nuggets of information you will never use again after graduating. But like "leave it" or "stay," learning about explanatory parentheticals is information you *will* use—if you ever submit your writing to a court.

What is an explanatory parenthetical?[1] It is information that you provide to a court about a case or cases, but you include the information

---

1. Broadly speaking, parentheticals can include many types of information that is placed within parentheses, and if you look at the *Bluebook* index under "parenthetical indications," you will find almost three columns of references to parentheses use in various

inside parentheses instead of talking about a case in a fuller paragraph. Here is one (fictional) example:

> *State v. Smith*, 16 P.3d 25, 28 (Ariz. 2010) (holding that laches did not bar an equitable claim filed four years after the wrongdoing was discovered).

In the above example, the information contained within the parentheses is what is called an "explanatory parenthetical."

Knowing how and when to craft an explanatory parenthetical is a critical skill for legal writers for many reasons. First, judges like seeing them in your written work. Justice Ginsburg, in one of her many articles about appellate advocacy, included "parenthetical explanations" in her "check list for a first-rate brief."[2] Leonard Garth, formerly Senior Judge on the Third Circuit, was even more emphatic: "The single, easiest way to make a good brief better is by the judicious use of parentheticals following case citations. There is nothing more frustrating than a brief that spends 15 pages discussing every detail of every case tangentially related to the real question at issue."[3] Similarly, in a survey conducted in 2018 of more than a thousand state and federal judges at all levels, judges "rail[ed]" against lawyers including too many quotations and facts when discussing other cases when it would have been more effective to include a parenthetical.[4]

Second, crafting a parenthetical and using it correctly will prove to your audience that you not only understand the complexities in the law,

---

legal-writing scenarios. THE BLUEBOOK: A UNIFORM SYSTEM OF CITATION at 352–53 (Columbia L. Rev. Ass'n et al. eds, 21st ed. 2020) [hereinafter BLUEBOOK]. This chapter, however, is limited to parentheticals where substantive information is included about caselaw, as opposed to items such as indicating that the opinion was per curiam or that a judge was dissenting and similar types of information. *See also* CAROLYN V. WILLIAMS, ASS'N OF LEGAL WRITING DIRS., ALWD GUIDE TO LEGAL CITATION 385 (Wolters Kluwer 7th ed.) [hereinafter ALWD] (describing an "explanatory parenthetical" as unlike other types of parentheticals because it is optional and is added "as a service to the reader.").

2. Ruth B. Ginsburg, *Remarks on Appellate Advocacy*, 50 S. C. L. Rev. 567, 568 (1999).

3. Leonard I. Garth, *How to Appeal to an Appellate Judge*, LITIGATION, Fall 1994, at 20, 24.

4. Ross Guberman, *Judges Speaking Softly: What They Long for When They Read*, LITIGATION, Summer 2018, at 48, 51. To be clear, however, judges also complained that in complex or dispositive cases, lawyers used parentheticals when a more robust textual illustration would have been appropriate. *Id.*

but are also able to write about the law clearly and concisely.[5] To draft an effective parenthetical, you have to understand where this authority fits into the overall argument, prove to the court that the cited authority supports the proposition to an unfamiliar reader, and do that all with limited words—so each word matters.[6]

Third, the judicious use of parentheticals can enhance your credibility with the court.[7] Drafting a parenthetical requires you to explain the holding and/or reasoning of a case in just a line or two, so if you can do it well, that shows your audience that you have command of the law and can be trusted to convey it accurately to the court.[8]

Thus, while there are detractors,[9] the overwhelming view is that explanatory parentheticals are critical to effective writing if used correctly.

All these reasons assume, however, that you know how to use them correctly. Because like handling fireworks on July 4th, the result could be a powerful colorful display, but if you mishandle them, the result could be bad. Your first task, therefore, is to figure out whether to use

---

5. Laurie A. Lewis, *The Stellar Parenthetical Illustration: A Tool to Open Doors in a Tight Job Market*, 19 PERSPS.: TEACHING LEGAL RSCH. & WRITING 35, 35 (2010).

6. *See* Eric P. Voigt, *Explanatory Parentheticals Can Pack a Persuasive Punch*, 45 MCGEORGE L. REV. 269, 273 (2013); Lewis, *supra* note 5, at 37–38.

7. *E.g.*, Voigt, *supra* note 6, at 275; THE WRITING CTR., GEORGETOWN UNIV. L. CTR., PARENTHETICALS 1 (2016). https://www.law.georgetown.edu/wp-content/uploads/2018/07/Parentheticals-Bluebook-Handout-Revision-Karl-Bock-2016.pdf ("Using parentheticals can often enhance your credibility with your legal audience.").

8. Voigt, *supra* note 6, at 276–77. In addition to these reasons, the proper use of parentheticals can make it less likely that you misrepresent the law. *Id.* at 277–78. Further, one legal writing expert has suggested that using parentheticals in a writing sample can help you get a job because doing so will make you stand out among other applicants. Lewis, *supra* note 5, at 39–41.

9. Bryan Garner criticized the use of parentheticals in an article written in the *ABA Journal*, but his criticism was directed at practitioners going overboard and using too many parentheticals without ever discussing case law contextually in actual paragraphs. Bryan A. Garner, *Parenthetical Habits: On the Use and Overuse of Parentheses and Brackets*, ABA J. (Nov. 1, 2016, 2:10 AM), https://www.abajournal.com/magazine/article/garner_parenthetical_habits; *see also* Eric B. Wolff, Appellate Tip-Stop with the Explanatory Parentheticals (Please), PERKINS COIE (OCT. 2019), https://www.perkinscoie.com/en/news-insights/appellate-tip-stop-with-the-explanatory-parentheticals-please.html (suggesting that practitioners should reduce their reliance on parentheticals, as it might be "a shortcut masquerading as helpfulness.").

an explanatory parenthetical or a more robust case illustration in your memo or brief.

A. The Power of the Story

As lawyers, we are engaged in rule-based analysis, but the problem is that cognitive theory teaches us that the "human brain does not effectively process abstract rules."[10] To understand these abstract rules, the human mind needs to associate them with stories or narratives.

We do this every day when we impart information. Let's say that your roommate is a slob, and you want to tell someone about that. You could just say, "My roommate is a slob." But that statement alone is not going to prove your point. You need to tell the story of the messy roommate. You therefore create a narrative with specific information proving that your roommate is a slob—someone who leaves dirty dishes in the sink, someone who leaves clothes on the floor of the living room, someone who leaves globs of toothpaste in the bathroom sink, and someone who allows the cat to pee on the carpet. This additional information helps illustrate the basic proposition: your roommate is a slob. You have proven your point through an illustration, and no one will judge you if you get a new roommate.

So, just as the bedtime stories our parents told helped us understand the world, the stories we tell in our legal documents help our readers understand the law.

What are the reasons we are called upon to illustrate an abstract rule? Michael Smith, in *Advanced Legal Writing*, provides these four classifications: elucidation, elimination, accentuation, and affiliation.[11]

The most important function for an illustration of a rule is elucidation—to explain a legal concept that is complex and ambiguous. Many legal rules fall into this category. For example, "nominative fair use" is a defense to a trademark infringement claim. No one is going to say upon learning that, "oh, I get it—no need to say anything further." A further explanation is needed.

---

10. MICHAEL R. SMITH, ADVANCED LEGAL WRITING 38 (Wolters Kluwer 3rd ed. 2013).

11. SMITH, *supra* note 10, at 41–47.

Here is an example of an explanation of just one of the elements needed to prove the defense:

> The defense is applicable if the defendant used "only so much of the mark…as is reasonably necessary to identify the…product or service." *Cairns v. Franklin Mint Co.*, 292 F.3d 1139, 1153 (9th Cir. 2002). What is "reasonably necessary" differs from case to case. *Id.* at 1154. For example, the Ninth Circuit found that the second element was met, despite a prominent reference to the trademark, because that reference was reasonably necessary for a customer to identify the defendant's product. *Id.* There, the plaintiff was a memorial fund established after Princess Diana's death to accept donations. *Id.* at 1144. Princess Diana's estate had authorized the fund to use Diana's name and likeness but had not authorized the defendant to do so. *Id.* In describing its products, the defendant used a caption that read "Diana" and showed a photograph of Diana wearing her royal tiara and bolero jacket. *Id.* at 1154. Finding the second element was met, the court reasoned: "In a nutshell, [the defendant] had to ensure that its customers understood the references to Princess Diana, and it did what was 'reasonably necessary' for this purpose." *Id.*
>
> Moreover, with respect to musical bands, courts generally find that the second element is met so long as the defendant has not used the band's logo. *The New Kids on the Block v. News Am. Publ'g, Inc.*, 971 F.2d 302, 308 (9th Cir. 1992) (stating that the defendants "do not use the New Kids' distinctive logo or anything else that isn't needed to make the announcements intelligible to readers); *Brother Records, Inc. v. Jardine*, 318 F.3d 900, 908 (9th Cir. 2003) (stating that "[the plaintiff] does not allege that [the defendant] uses any distinctive logo or 'anything else that isn't needed' to identify the Beach Boys, and [the defendant] therefore satisfies the second element.").

Because both the nominative fair use defense and one of its elements are not self-explanatory, a further illustration is needed, as shown above.

The second function of a narrative illustration is elimination; the writer wants to erase possible misinterpretations of the rule. A good example of this is the "actual physical control" requirement in statutes prohibiting driving under the influence. Vermont, as an example, provides that a person shall not be "in actual physical control of any vehicle... under the influence of intoxicating liquor."[12] Someone reading that statute might assume that the person driving must be in control of the vehicle and could not be liable, for example, if sleeping behind the wheel. That assumption, however, is wrong. Here is an illustration of the point:

> Actual physical control is found when a person has the "immediate potential to operate" a vehicle. *State v. Trucott*, 487 A.2d 149, 154 (Vt. 1984). The defendant's "*potential*, not the *intent*, to operate" is the key consideration for courts. *State v. Kelton*, 724 A.2d 452, 453 (Vt. 1998). Actual physical control can be present even if a defendant's diminished capacity precludes him from driving the car. *State v. Godfrey*, 400 A.2d 1026, 1026–27 (Vt. 1979). In *Godfrey*, the Court held the defendant was in actual physical control even though he was asleep behind the wheel of his vehicle. *Id.* at 1026. The defendant argued that because he was not touching "any mechanism by which the vehicle could be controlled," he could not be in actual physical control. *Id.* The Court reasoned that this argument, when taken to the extreme, would free the defendant from liability "if, seated at the controls of a car careening down the highway, he did not touch any of the controls." *Id.* at 1027. Rejecting the argument and its consequences, the Court explained that the defendant's reasoning amounted to "the use of diminished capacity (i.e. intoxication) to eliminate an element of specific intent." *Id.*

The third function of a case illustration is accentuation; the writer wants to "emphasize the operative effect of a general rule."[13] For example, in Mississippi, a notice of appeal must be filed within 30 days.[14] The writer wants to prove that this time limit is strictly construed, so there is

---

12. Vt. Stat. Ann. tit. 23, § 1201(a)(2) (West 2022).

13. Smith, *supra* note 10, at 46.

14. Miss. R. App. Proc. 4(a).

no wiggle room. One way to do this is to discuss a case where the court dismissed the appeal because the notice was filed a mere two days late.[15]

The final function for an illustrative narrative is affiliation—explaining a rule in more familiar terms.[16] Let's take the requirement that a plaintiff must have "standing" to sue someone. Does this mean you have to be standing up when suing someone? Of course not. So the term "standing" requires an explanation. Standing is the legal concept which addresses whether a party has the right to bring a lawsuit in a particular case. For example, in *Sierra Club v. Hawai'i Tourism Authority*,[17] a national conservation group challenged the Hawai'i Tourism Authority's decision to contract for tourism marketing services without conducting an environmental assessment. The issue was whether the group had "standing" to sue. The Hawaii Supreme Court held it did not because it could not show: (1) that it would suffer an actual or threatened injury because of the marketing services proposed in the contract; (2) that the alleged or threatened injury was fairly traceable to expenditures for such services; and (3) that any such injury would likely be remedied by a favorable judicial decision.[18]

Now that we understand the purposes of illustrating abstract rules and the reasons behind doing so, it is time to learn how and when to use a parenthetical to help tell your story. Unfortunately, there are no hard and fast rules, so this is where your critical thinking and analysis come into play in assessing several factors. Think of a parenthetical as a very short story to illustrate a rule. In contrast, a full case illustration in your brief is more like a novel. Do you need a novel or a novella?[19]

There are a few considerations, so ask yourself these questions:[20]

---

15. Tandy Elec. Inc. v. Fletcher, 554 So. 2d 308, 308, 312 (Miss. 1989) (dismissing an appeal filed 32 days after entry of judgment where the limit to file a notice of appeal was 30 days).

16. SMITH, *supra* note 10, at 45.

17. 59 P.3d 877 (Haw. 2002).

18. *Id.* at 880.

19. The other alternative is that the rule is so straightforward that you do not need a parenthetical or a case illustration. For example, a two-year statute of limitations for negligence arising out of car accident is so plain and simple that no further explanation (other than a cite to the applicable statute) is needed.

20. *See* SMITH, *supra* note 10, at 51–52.

1. Is the rule critical to the outcome of your case? If so, a more robust illustration is probably needed.
2. Is the rule just one part of a multi-factor test or is it the entire
   test? If it is just one part of a multi-factor test that does not control the outcome, then that would weigh toward a less robust illustration, and a parenthetical might be sufficient.
3. Is the rule complex and ambiguous? If so, that would be a reason
   to use a more robust explanation of the law.
4. Do you have concerns about the length of your document? If so,
   and you are trying to squeeze in information where you may
   already be close to the word limit, this too will be a consideration.

Sometimes, you may determine that you need neither a robust illustration nor a parenthetical to explain a rule. For example, the standard
for granting a summary judgment motion is so well known that, beyond
citing to the rule of procedure, there is usually no reason to include a
case illustration or a parenthetical.[21]

B. Examples of Effective Parentheticals

Before we talk about mistakes students (and lawyers) commonly
make when drafting parentheticals, let's look at some effective examples
of parentheticals.

Let's take a brief submitted recently to the United States Supreme
Court by the Solicitor General's Office (as amicus curiae) in *Mahanoy
Area School District v. B.L.*[22] In *Mahanoy Area School District*, the issue

---

21. Voigt, *supra* note 6, at 278. There are some exceptions to this rule, however, especially for less-well-known claims where it might be important for a court to see some
examples of cases where summary judgment has been entered if it would otherwise not
be obvious.

22. Brief for United States as Amicus Curiae Supporting Petitioner, Mahanoy Sch.
Dist. v. B.L., 141 S. Ct. 2038 (2021) (No. 20-255), 2021 WL 859695. Note that the student won in this case, so the petitioner school (who the United States was supporting)
lost. Nonetheless, the school did not lose due to the use of parentheticals in the Solicitor
General's brief, and it is a good example of effective legal writing. In fact, one of the best
places to find examples of excellent legal writing is the website linking briefs prepared
by the Solicitor General of the United States because those briefs are well written and
provide good examples for your own writing. *A Great Source for Sample Appellate Briefs,*

involved a high school student who was removed from the cheerleading team because of two messages she posted on social media after not making the varsity squad.[23] These messages contained curse words. The issue was whether the public school had the authority to discipline her for speech occurring off campus or whether this trampled on the student's First Amendment rights.

In its brief supporting the school, the Solicitor General's Office made liberal use of parentheticals throughout. One tactic you can find in the brief is selective quoting from cases and placing those quotations in parentheticals, like this:

> Because the task of educating the Nation's children vests public schools with responsibility to teach students, a school may prohibit student speech that "would undermine the school's basic educational mission." *Fraser*, 478 U.S. at 685; *see Kuhlmeier*, 484 U.S. at 266 ("A school need not tolerate student speech that is inconsistent with its 'basic educational mission,' even though the government could not censor similar speech outside the school.") (quoting *Fraser*, 478 U.S. at 685).[24]

Note that the parenthetical is not used alone to support the point but after the lawyers have set forth the general proposition in text.

Parentheticals are also used to briefly summarize holdings of cases to support a broad legal proposition about the law after first stating the proposition, as in the passage below:

> When school administrators are alerted to messages by a student that, for instance, suggest plans for violence, they cannot be said to have violated the First Amendment when they take reasonable steps to avert that potential harm. *See, e.g., McNeil v. Sherwood School District 88J*, 918 F.3d 700, 703–704 (9th Cir. 2019) (per curiam) (upholding one-year expulsion of a student with "access to firearms" who created "a hit list of students" who "'must die'"); *Wynar v. Douglas County School District*, 728 F.3d

---

LEGAL WRITING PROF BLOG (Jan. 9, 2017), https://lawprofessors.typepad.com/legalwriting/2017/01/a-great-source-for-sample-appellate-briefs.html.

23. 141 S. Ct. at 2043.

24. Brief for the United States, *supra* note 22, at 9, 2021 WL 859695, at *9.

1062, 1070 (9th Cir. 2013) (upholding temporary expulsion of a student "with confirmed access to weapons" who posted social-media "messages that could be interpreted as a plan to attack the school" and that were "brought to the school's attention by fellow students"); *Wisniewski v. Board of Education*, 494 F.3d 34, 36 (2d Cir. 2007) (upholding suspension of student who circulated an instant-messenger icon depicting "a pistol firing a bullet at a person's head, above which were dots representing splattered blood," and below which were the words "'Kill Mr. VanderMolen,'" an English teacher at the school), cert. denied, 552 U.S. 1296 (2008).[25]

Although the above example includes holdings only, there is no requirement that parentheticals only include holdings. Take this example in the same brief, which refers to the Supreme Court "recognizing" a principle as opposed to holding something:

> Restrictions applied to school speech in that context should be reasonable and tied to safeguarding, or preventing the substantial undermining of, an essential or inherent feature of the program, in service of both the success of the program and the safety of its participants. It is relevant as well whether a student who objects to such conditions can forgo participation in that particular program. *Cf. Alliance for Open Society*, 570 U.S. at 214; *Vernonia*, 515 U.S. at 657 (recognizing that "students who voluntarily participate in school athletics have reason to expect intrusions upon normal rights and privileges" even beyond those intrusions "imposed on students generally").[26]

Another common use of parentheticals in this brief is after a signal, such as *Cf.* or *See also.*[27] The parenthetical is used where the relevance of the authority might not otherwise be clear, as in the following passage:

---

25. *Id.* at 15–16, 2021 WL 859695 at *15–16.

26. *Id.* at 30, 2021 WL 859695 at *30.

27. If you have not already learned about signals, you will soon. A signal prefaces a citation to indicate "the type and degree of support or contradiction the cited authority provides for a proposition in text." ALWD, *supra* note 1, at 370.

Off-campus speech—including speech communicated via email, text message, social media, and the like—that is harassing or bullying can contribute to depriving victims of the educational opportunities to which they are entitled. Under those circumstances, school officials attempting to satisfy their obligations under federal law to address those harms should not be placed in the difficult position of having to blind themselves to instances of the harassing or bullying conduct that occurred online. *Cf. Tinker*, 393 U.S. at 513 (observing that student speech or conduct, "in class or out of it," that involves "invasion of the rights of others" is "not immunized by the constitutional guarantee of freedom of speech"); *Feminist Majority Foundation v. Hurley*, 911 F.3d 674, 688–689 (4th Cir. 2018) ("[W]e cannot conclude that [the school] could turn a blind eye to the sexual harassment that pervaded and disrupted its campus solely because the offending conduct took place through cyberspace.").[28]

C. Common Mistakes

Now that you have seen some examples of effective parentheticals, you might be thinking that seems straightforward, and no one could make a mistake. But parentheticals are trickier than you might expect. Especially when first learning about parentheticals, make sure you avoid making these common mistakes.

First, do not assume that a parenthetical is always the best way to go. It isn't. I say this because in my experience, when students first learn about parentheticals, they get addicted and think, "Wow, these are cool; I think I will place them everywhere, no matter what the situation calls for." Use them sensibly.

For example, if there is a rule that governs your case, and it is contained either in a statute, a rule, or a case, do not bury the rule in a parenthetical. Information in a parenthetical is, by definition, not as important as information contained in the text of your discussion, so use a parenthetical to supplement information about the rule only.[29]

---

28. Brief for the United States, *supra* note 22, at 18, 2021 WL 859695, at *18.
29. Smith, *supra* note 10, at 59.

Here is an effective example:

> The majority of courts have held that a variety of non-contract tort claims not rising to the level of a trade secret are preempt-ed, including the exact claims made here. *Smith v. Jones*, 35 P.3d 36 (Ala. 2003) (preempting claims for unjust enrichment and conversion); *Springer v. Smith*, 36 P.3d 36 (Mont. 2008) (pre-empting claims for unfair competition and conversion); *Harris v. Lookout*, 36 P.3d 56 (Wash. 2009) (preempting claims for un-fair competition, breach of the duty of good faith and fair deal-ing, and unjust enrichment).

Similarly, once you have stated the rule, there is no reason to restate it in a parenthetical. This is simply repetitive and unnecessary because it adds nothing. Your goal is not to show your reader how many cases you can find that say the exact same thing.

Further, even if your intent is not to restate a general rule, you might end up doing so unintentionally because you have worded the paren-thetical in overly broad terms.

Here is an example:

> The majority of courts have held that non-contract tort claims not rising to the level of a trade secret are preempted, including the exact claims made here. *Smith v. Jones*, 35 P.3d 36 (Ala. 2003) (preempting claims).

In the above example, you would eliminate the parenthetical and replace it with parentheticals that do a better job of proving the point, such as the example listed above where the types of claims courts have dismissed are specified.

Another common mistake is to draft overly long parentheticals. One rule of thumb is to make sure a parenthetical is no longer than one sen-tence.[30] In fact, one legal writing expert, comparing a parenthetical to Twitter, recommends using no more than 280 characters.[31] If it is long

---

30. Smith, *supra* note 10, at 61.

31. Nick Wagoner, *Common Parenthetical Pitfalls*, Legal Skills Prof Blog (Jan. 19, 2012), https://lawprofessors.typepad.com/legal_skills/2012/01/guest-blogger-nick-wag-oner-on-common-parenthetical-pitfalls.html.

and rambling, that is an indication that you should discuss the case in text instead of in a parenthetical.

Here is an example of a rambling parenthetical:

> A majority of courts have held that the UTSA preempts common-law tort claims not rising to the level of a trade secret. *Smith v. Jones*, 25 P.3d at 26 (holding that the plain language is clear under the act because there is only one way to construe it. The language is "plain and clear" that tort claims not rising to the level of a trade secret have to be preempted under the two-tiered approach described in the legislative history of the Act—the two tiers being protected information and general unprotected information that deserves no protection at all; any other result would be "absurd").

Sometimes, students (and lawyers) will also make the mistake of using the word *holding* when, in fact, the information is not a holding, thereby hurting the writer's credibility. Keep handy a helpful laundry list of words that can be used instead of holding, such as adopting, allowing, analyzing, applying, approving, awarding, construing, determining, indicating, recognizing, or rejecting.[32] (Maybe make a magnet with these words on it and then put it on your refrigerator along with those wedding invitations.) In other words, think carefully before choosing that present participle[33] to make sure it accurately reflects a court's actions.

The final mistake students make is instead of using a *present participle*, such as *holding*, incorrectly using a *gerund* instead (a form of a verb that really functions as a noun), an "ing" word that relates to the parties instead of a court's action in deciding a case.[34]

Here is an example:

> Florida courts also consider in determining whether a worker is an "employee" or an "independent contractor" who supplies the worker's tools. If workers supply their own tools, this factor will support a finding that the worker is an independent contractor. *See, e.g., Kane Furniture Corp. v. Miranda*, 506 So.2d

---

32. Voigt, *supra* note 6, at 282 n.55.
33. A present participle is a form of a verb ending in "ing."
34. SMITH, *supra* note 10, at 62.

1061, 1065 (Fla. Dist. Ct. App. 1987) (supplying his own instal-
lation equipment in performing his work supported a finding
that a carpet installer was an independent contractor).[35]

The use of the word "supplying" in the above parenthetical is inaccurate
because it refers to the one of the parties instead of the court.

The reasoning behind using a present participle is that it immediately
identifies the court's action. If a present participle were not used, the
reader might perceive the information to be the writer's own thoughts,
which carry no weight.[36]

D. Style Guidelines for Parentheticals

While no one can give you hard and fast rules for when to use parentheticals because it depends on the context, there are some general style
guidelines you should follow when drafting parentheticals.

First, as mentioned above, when you use a signal in your memo
or brief, you should consider using a parenthetical. *Bluebook* and the
ALWD Guide both provide recommendations on whether you should
use an explanatory parenthetical or not depending on what signal you
use. Here is a handy chart that summarizes the information:[37]

No Parentheticals	Parentheticals Encouraged	Parentheticals Strongly Recommended
E.g.,	See also	Cf.
See	See generally	Compare... with...
Accord		But cf.
Contra		
But see		

Even though these guides contain helpful recommendations, ultimately, you should decide whether an explanatory parenthetical would
be helpful to your reader even if one of these style guides does not rec-

---

35. *Id.*
36. Voigt, *supra* note 6, at 282.
37. *See* BLUEBOOK, *supra* note 1, at 62–63; ALWD, *supra* note 1, at 370–72.

ommend one. For example, if you look at the Solicitor General's brief quoted above, you will notice that the authors used explanatory parentheticals for certain signals (such as *see* and *e.g.*), even though the style guides recommend against doing so.

Second, keep in mind that if you are beginning your parenthetical with a present participle (as you will frequently), such as "holding," or "finding," then your phrase is not a complete sentence, so you do not capitalize the first word, and you do not put a period at the end inside the parentheses. Instead, a period goes after the closing parenthesis (or that period might be a semicolon if you are including more than one parenthetical).[38]

Third, the rule immediately above on capitalization does not apply if you are quoting from a case. In that event, use the capitalization and punctuation in the original quotation—unless you are altering the quotation for some reason. If the quotation is a full sentence, then you will capitalize the first letter, and the period will go inside the parentheses (and then you need another period outside the parentheses). If you are only including a partial quotation, you can begin with a lowercase letter and end with no closing punctuation.

Finally, advice on whether to include articles, such as "the," "a," "an," etc., is mixed. The *Bluebook* and the *ALWD Guide* agree that you can omit extraneous words such as "the" unless doing so would cause confusion.[39] However, other style guides give writers different advice. The *Yale Law Journal Style Guide* provides that writers "should… include articles (e.g., "a," "the") in parentheticals whenever you would use them in ordinary sentences."[40] Similarly, The University of Chicago's Manual of Legal Citation, the *Maroonbook*, provides that articles should not be omitted from parentheticals.[41] In fact, Smith, in his textbook on advanced legal

---

38. Bryan A. Garner, The Redbook: A Manual on Legal Style 177 (4th ed. 2018).

39. Bluebook, *supra* note 1, at 65; ALWD, *supra* note 1, at 387.

40. Yale L.J., Volume 131 Style Guide 5 (2021), https://www.yalelawjournal.org/files/Volume131StyleGuide_pydp1jqn.pdf.

41. Univ. of Chi. L. Rev., The Maroonbook 10 (2019), https://lawreview.uchicago.edu/sites/lawreview.uchicago.edu/files/v87%20Maroonbook.pdf.

writing, goes so far as to place omission of articles in a parenthetical as one of the common mistakes made in crafting parentheticals.[42]

Here are examples of parentheticals with and without articles:[43]

> Without articles: The employment handbooks in the two cases cited by Plaintiff contained no disclaimer stating that employment was at will: unsurprisingly, those courts determined that the handbooks altered the at-will status of those employees. *See Paniagua v. City of Galveston*, 995 F.2d 1310, 1314-15 (5th Cir. 1993) (relying on "absence of any disclaimer" in concluding that employee's claim was valid); *Vida v. El Paso Employees' Fed. Credit Union*, 885 S.W. 2d 177, 180–81 (Tex. Ct. App. 1994) (ruling that handbook lacking disclaimer altered plaintiff's at-will employment).

> With articles: The employment handbooks in the two cases cited by Plaintiff contained no disclaimer stating that employment was at will: unsurprisingly, those courts determined that the handbooks altered the at-will status of those employees. *See Paniagua v. City of Galveston*, 995 F.2d 1310, 1314–15 (5th Cir. 1993) (relying on **the** "absence of any disclaimer" in concluding that **the** employee's claim was valid); *Vida v. El Paso Employees' Fed. Credit Union*, 885 S.W. 2d 177, 180–81 (Tex. Ct. App. 1994) (ruling that **the** handbook lacking **any** disclaimer altered **the** plaintiff's at-will employment).

It is at this point that my students would say something like, "Just tell us what you want us to do." In my opinion, if you have room, include articles. I do not think anyone would judge you for including them, but there is a chance someone might judge you for not including them. Your reader might think that you do not know where articles are needed or

---

42. Smith, *supra* note 10, at 61. His rationale is that while omitting articles might save space, failure to follow standard grammatical rules "distracts readers. The small amount of space saved by omitting articles does not justify the distraction such omissions cause to readers." *Id.* at 62.

43. These examples are taken from Voigt, *supra* note 6, at 301, although the author used them to make a different point about using parentheticals to distinguish adverse authorities.

think that the meaning is unclear without them, even though you think the meaning is clear (and one thing we know is that it does not matter what you think but what your audience thinks). But if your audience wants you to omit articles, follow that advice, as your audience is always what matters.

Like the "stay" and "leave it" commands, explanatory parentheticals are a valuable tool in any legal writer's toolbox. Think carefully about when to use them and what information to include about the cases, and then make sure you follow the style guidelines in doing so. If you can do all of that, you will stand out as an effective legal writer, and your supervisors (and later, the courts you appear before) will be pleased.

Index